HIGHER EDUCATION IN SUB-SAHARAN AFRICA

HIGHER EDUCATION IN SUB-SAHARAN AFRICA

KEITH HINCHLIFFE

CROOM HELM
London • Sydney • Wolfeboro, New Hampshire

Croom Helm Ltd., Provident House, Burrell Row,
Beckenham, Kent BR3 1AT
Croom Helm Australia, 44-50 Waterloo Road,
North Ryde, 2113, New South Wales

British Library Cataloguing in Publication Data
Hinchliffe, Keith
    Higher education in sub-Saharan Africa.
    1. Education, Higher — Africa, Sub-Saharan
    I. Title
    378.67   LA2090.A357
    ISBN 0-7099-3783-0

Croom Helm, 27 South Main Street, Wolfeboro,
New Hampshire 03894-2069 USA

Library of Congress Cataloging in Publication Data
applied for:

591 92/89

Printed and bound in Great Britain
by Billing & Sons Limited, Worcester.

Contents

Tables

This book is dedicated to my mother for her love and support and to the memory of a dog called Rupert

1 Introduction

The majority of sub Saharan African countries gained political independence between 1957 and 1964. Economic, political and social factors at that time led to a major emphasis being placed on the rapid development of the educational system. Since then, continuing pressures in the form of both student and labour market demand plus the internal expansionary logic of education systems have combined to ensure that rates of growth of enrolments have been well above population growth rates and that in all African countries the sector receives the largest slice of government expenditure, apart from the military in particular cases. These expansionary pressures are increasingly meeting a severe financial constraint. Since neither the pressures nor the constraints are likely to relent of their own accord in the foreseeable future, policies are required to either slow down student demand, ensure that additional demand is met at a constant quality at lower unit cost through increased efficiency, or increase resources.

The separate levels of education form one whole system with graduates of each feeding the next and to a certain extent determining the quality at that level. What can be achieved at each level depends in part on what was achieved at the previous one. Flows also occur in the opposite direction as graduates of higher levels become teachers at lower levels and again, in part, determine the quality of that education. In these ways the various levels of education are complementary. In other ways, however, they may be competitive in that they may each compete for a share of a given education budget. In such a case, any expansion of a given level leads to a lower degree of expansion elsewhere than could otherwise have been attained.

Enrolments in higher education in sub Saharan African countries have increased by over 11 percent a year since 1960. While these remain under one percent of total educational enrolments they consume, on average, almost 20 percent of central governments' educational expenditures.

1

Currently the higher education sector is subject to a number of critiques in terms of its role in society, the effectiveness of its teaching, the use which can be made of its graduates, the level of costs per graduate and the overall return on the resources consumed. Much of this critique has been based on very scattered and partial evidence and on the presumption that experiences in less developed countries in other parts of the world can be generalised to Africa. This book attempts to partly rectify this situation by bringing together a wide range of material on higher education in Africa, focussing particularly on the present and future short-term nature of the labour market facing university graduates and on the level and composition of unit costs. Much of the discussion is placed in the context of an expected severe constraint on government finance in the foreseeable future.

Following this Introduction, chapter 2 begins with a rapid description of the trends and levels of educational enrolments and expenditures over the past twenty-five years or so in sub Saharan African countries. This is followed by a discussion of some of the economic and social effects of primary and secondary schooling in the region, focussing on labour incomes and changes in fertility and mortality patterns. The rest of the book is devoted to higher education and to the universities in particular. In chapter 3 the initial roles perceived for the universities in sub Saharan Africa together with their growth and current status are described. This chapter is particularly important as a base for later discussions of the costs and outputs of the universities since to a large extent the decisions made in the 1950s and 1960s about the appropriate nature of post-secondary education institutions, and the roles they would and should play, have had a lasting effect. Since their establishment, the universities in Africa have had their critics and, if anything, the numbers are growing. In the final part of chapter 3, the criticisms are briefly presented.

The following four chapters take up in detail some of the issues raised in chapter 3. Chapter 4 concentrates on the efficiency with which the universities prepare students for the labour market and attempts to assess the appropriateness of both the total size and the distribution of enrolments in African countries. Discussion ranges over manpower forecasts and evaluations of these methods of assessing shortages and surpluses, the responses of the universities to changing labour demands and possible reforms to secure a tighter meshing of supply and demand. On the basis of a wide range of information covering rates of return, wage trends, levels of expatriate employment,

2

vacancies and so on, summaries of labour market conditions are built up for sixteen individual countries. Turning to research, this is a particularly difficult aspect to evaluate, but some changes to present arrangements and suggestions for strengthening particular aspects are presented.

In the first of three chapters focussing on costs, chapter 5 concentrates on the current constraints surrounding government financing of higher education and on the increasing social demand for this level of education. Two policies suggest themselves - reductions in costs and additional non-government finance. Chapter 6 deals widely with the internal efficiency of universities. Unit costs are presented for a large number of institutions and their determinants are documented through case studies. Student wastage rates are then assembled. The second half of the chapter concentrates on the feasibility of reducing costs while affecting teaching quality as little as possible. In the last of the general chapters, the possibilities of increasing non-government levels of finance are discussed. In particular, current student financing arrangements are documented and the arguments surrounding the issue of increased student contributions through charges and/or loans are presented. The feasibility of loans are judged through case studies and simulations.

Chapter 8 contains extensive case studies of university development, costs and financing in Ghana and Nigeria. Though sharing many features in their early years, the university systems of the two countries have evolved very differently in size and cost since the late 1960s. In Ghana, enrolments and finance have largely stagnated whereas in Nigeria, until recently, enrolments doubled every four years and the number of universities continued to grow. Currently, however, the sector in each country is being required to operate at far lower levels of funding than in the past and below those which they were designed to use. In comparison with other levels of education, however, and levels of domestic resources, the universities in these countries remain very expensive and it is argued that they are simultaneously under- and over-financed. This apparent contradiction arises from the very high levels of expenditure on functions other than teaching and research resulting from the conceptions of the purpose of universities initially adopted in the 1950s. Separating out and analysing the various components, it is argued, enables the question of the appropriate source of funding for the non-academic functions to be more seriously faced. This is done for the universities in both countries.

In the final chapter, the conclusions derived from

both the general survey of university development in sub Saharan Africa and the case studies are presented. The universities, generally, are not in good shape. For whatever reason, they are short of funds in relation to the functions they are required to carry out. Either funds must increase or the functions must be reduced. The alternative of reduced government funds with no reassessment of their use or measures to augment them will ensure a further deterioration in the quality of higher education.

At the outset of this study it needs to be made clear that this is not an encyclopedic account of higher education in all sub Saharan African countries. While some documentation has been located for most countries, the extent is uneven. The book is issue oriented and built up from case studies. However, there is reason to believe that the issues that recurringly arise in the universities in those countries for which documentation is relatively extensive can be generalised.

2 Schooling in
sub Saharan Africa

In the Introduction it was argued that in various ways the separate levels of education inter-relate and form one whole system. However, all the chapters following this one concentrate on higher education, particularly the universities, and apart from some comparisons of unit costs and discussion of problems in university science departments resulting from poor science teaching in schools, little direct attention is given to primary and secondary schooling. This chapter partially fills the obvious gap. It is divided into two sections and begins by briefly describing the levels and growth of enrolments and education expenditures across the whole education system in sub Saharan African countries. This is followed by a discussion of some of the effects of primary and secondary education. The effects concentrated on are economic production and demographic change. Readers who are aware of these issues or simply prefer to go straight into a discussion of higher education can omit this second section and move to chapter 3 without losing continuity.

ENROLMENT GROWTH AND EDUCATION EXPENDITURES

Over the past 25 years enrolments in education in sub Saharan Africa countries have increased substantially. Between 1960 and 1970 enrolments grew at annual average rates of 5.4, 11.4 and 11.7 percent for primary, secondary and higher education respectively and for the period 1970 to 1980 at 7.3, 13.4 and 11.5 percent. In part, these differences in enrolment growth rates between primary and post-primary education reflect earlier periods of substantial primary enrolment growth and also reflect the concern with 'qualified manpower requirements' emphasised particularly in the 1960s. Because of high rates of population growth, rising to over 4 percent a year in Kenya, increases in enrolment ratios have been less dramatic than might have been expected. Between 1960 and 1980, the average enrolment ratio for primary rose from 36 percent to 60 percent, secondary from 3 percent to 14 per—

cent and for higher from almost zero to 1.4 percent. These averages hide wide variations. Table 2.1 presents current enrolment ratios for a selected range of countries. The countries not only display differences in absolute enrolment ratios but also in their patterns of enrolments. The effects

Table 2.1.   Enrolment Ratios in Selected African Countries (percent)

Country	Primary	Secondary	Higher
Tanzania	98	3	0.3
Swaziland	93	29	3.0
Cameroon	74	14	1.3
Somalia	22	12	1.0
Mali	20	1	0.9
Niger	17	2	0.2

Source: World Bank (1985).

of different colonial powers on educational structures are still very evident. Separating sub Saharan African countries into English-speaking and French-speaking, it is very noticeable that primary education coverage is higher and post-secondary education coverage lower in the English-speaking countries. This is shown in table 2.2.

High growth rates of enrolment have necessitated large increases in expenditures. In many countries since 1960, public expenditures on education have grown faster than both gross national product and aggregate government expenditure. For all sub Saharan African countries combined, the share of education expenditure in gross national product rose from 3.2 percent in 1965 to 4.1 percent in 1980. Appendix Table A2 presents the shares of education expenditures in gross national product in a number of African countries around 1970 and 1980. Again for 1980, the average percentage of total government ex-

6

Table 2.2. Literacy Rates and Enrolment Ratios by
Level of Education, Africa (percent)

Country Group	Primary	Secondary	Higher	Adult Literacy
Francophone Africa	46	14	2.4	18
Anglophone Africa	77	17	1.2	40

Source: Mingat and Psacharopoulos (1984).

penditure spent on education in 36 countries was 18.9
ranging from 4 percent in Mauritius to 45 percent in the
Ivory Coast (Appendix Table A1).
     Within the overall increase in public expenditures on
education, the shares between levels have changed over
time reflecting both differences in rates of enrolment
growth and different rates of increase in unit costs.
Examples of changing shares between 1970 and 1980 are
documented in table 2.3. In all the cases illustrated, the
share for higher education has increased considerably.
Appendix Table A1 presents the current distribution for 30
countries. Averages are 50 percent for primary, 32 percent
for secondary and 18 percent for higher. Differences in
unit costs between students at different education levels in
Africa are substantial. On average, a year of secondary
schooling is four times as expensive as a year of primary
schooling and higher education is 40 times as expensive.
As is shown in chapter 6, these differences are much
greater than those in countries in other regions of the
world.
     In terms of students enrolled and expenditures made,
the education sector has been one of the most expansionist
sectors in sub Saharan Africa over recent decades. Its
appeal has been wide and large claims have been made
regarding its benefits. In the period of greatest optimism,
in the early 1960s, education was widely regarded as
capable of producing rapid economic growth, greater
equality between social and ethnic groups, stronger
feelings of national unity and in general was taken to be
the route to 'modernisation'. Over the last decade, a much

Table 2.3. Distribution of Educational Expenditure
by Level, 1970 and 1980 (percent)

Country	Year	Primary	Secondary	Higher
Botswana	1970	60	31	9
	1980	55	31	14
Congo	1970	52	38	10
	1980	41	32	27
Malawi	1970	47	26	27
	1980	49	19	32
Zambia	1970	51	34	15
	1980	51	29	20
Upper Volta	1970	46	28	26
	1980	38	23	39

Source: UNESCO (1983).

greater degree of scepticism has developed as economic
stagnation and civil wars have occurred widely across the
region. The dynamic of expansion inherent in educational
systems remains but there is less belief in its social
benefits. At the same time, declining government revenues
are resulting in pressures to slow down education
expansion and to reduce the resources for each pupil.
These trends are occurring in most countries and at all
levels of education.
    Both the optimism and the scepticism concerning
educational development in sub Saharan Africa have been
based on extremely scanty information, mostly qualitative,
and most views have been based on largely impressionistic
evidence. In the field of higher education this book
attempts to rectify, somewhat, this lack of quantitative
information by focussing in detail on both the costs
involved and the outcomes measured mainly in terms of
employment variables. Prior to the main discussion of high-

er education, however, the rest of this chapter focusses on the effects of primary and secondary schooling. Previous studies of the effects of schooling have largely concentrated on labour market outcomes, including levels of unemployment. In this chapter, recent employment studies are also described but they are supplemented by analyses of the effects of schooling on other aspects of social and economic behaviour. In particular, emphasis is placed on the effect of schooling on levels of fertility, child mortality and nutrition.

THE EFFECTS OF PRIMARY AND SECONDARY SCHOOLING

Twenty years ago, measures of the benefits of education concentrated mainly on the resulting increases in labour productivity in the formal wage earning sector. Today, as a result of both increased empirical knowledge and advances in theory, the benefits from education can begin to be placed in a wider overall framework. This section is divided into two parts both of which are based on data from sub Saharan African countries. The first is directly related to economic production and the effect of education on an individual's earnings and output. In addition to evidence from the formal wage earning sector over time, data from surveys in the urban informal sector and in farming are presented. In the second part, the effects of education on what may be broadly called health and demographic change are discussed. These are disaggregated into fertility and infant and child mortality. Better health is an end in itself. It also has a variety of direct and indirect economic implications.

Education and Economic Production

The economic effectiveness of schooling has commonly been judged by social rates of return. Put simply, these compare additional incomes said to be a measure of increased productivity attributable to schooling to the costs of schooling. In the most recent compilation of these rates of return from around the world, 16 African countries are covered (Psacharopoulos, 1985). Taking the most recent estimates for each country the average social rates of return are (in percent); primary 27, secondary 17 and higher 12.

Levels and patterns of rates of return to education can be powerful indicators of the economic efficiency with which resources are being used. The present studies for Africa suggest that while returns to all levels of education are high, compared to most other investments, they are the

9

highest at the lower levels. Most of these studies, however, suffer from data limitations and are in need of revision in at least two respects. First, many were made using earnings estimates which today are between ten and 20 years old. While these estimates may have reasonably reflected the state of the labour market at that time it is less likely that they reflect the present state. Second, the studies generally used earnings from only the formal wage earning sector (even for primary school leavers), most often assumed full employment and in some cases were simply based on government salary scales. Very few of the studies used cross sectional age-education-earnings survey data even confined to the formal sector.

More, and more careful, economy-wide earnings surveys are required, together with other labour market indicators, to provide a picture of the employment prospects of African school leavers in the 1980s and an assessment of the economic returns which can be expected from investment in the various levels of education. In the absence of such surveys, the types of data which have been used so far in the African rate of return studies are simply extended and added to in the following discussion. First, the results of recent work on earning structures and trends in the formal sector are discussed. These are then followed by some documentation of education-earning/output relationships in the urban informal sector and in the rural sector.

The Formal Sector. Two factors set the context for a discussion of formal sector employment in Africa. First, throughout the 1970s the public sector grew rapidly and currently dominates formal sector employment. Second, despite this growth, the proportions of the total labour force employed in the formal sector remain low. Table 2.4 demonstrates these points for seven countries.

The rather comforting picture of rapid expansion in the sector dominating the employment aspirations of school leavers in the 1970s is changing in the 1980s. Public sector employment expansion is slowing down considerably while the numbers of school graduates continue to increase. In several countries over the last few years employment guarantees have been rescinded, even for university graduates, and there is widespread pressure to stabilise rather than expand public employment. The Third National Development Plan of Zambia (1979-83) provides an example of the differences between expected new wage jobs and school graduates. At each level, graduates exceed wage jobs by a ratio of three or four to one. Similarly, Kenya's 1979-83 Development Plan envisaged some 60,000 new jobs

Table 2.4. Formal Sector and Public Employment in
           Selected African Countries

Country	Year	Formal Sector Employment As Percent Total Labour Force	Public Employment As Percent Formal Employment	Annual Growth Public Employment Percent 1970s
Gambia	1977	10.4	76.0	14.0
Ghana	1980	12.3	75.8	n.a
Kenya	1979	16.0	46.9	8.0
Liberia	1979	22.0	43.6	6.0
Somalia	1978	8.0	93.0	17.0
Tanzania	1976	7.3	67.0	n.a
Zambia	1976	24.0	71.6	n.a

Source: International Labour Office (1982) p.14:
          plus government and World Bank estimates.

compared to 68,000 leavers with full secondary schooling,
50,000 with junior secondary schooling and 100,000 with
primary schooling.
        As table 2.4 indicates, formal sector employment is
achieved only by a minority of all workers. The chances
of this type of employment, however, differ considerably by
educational level and are continually changing. In recent
years, studies have been made in Malawi, Swaziland and
Tanzania tracing the employment records of secondary
school leavers. These give some indication of changing
labour conditions.
        The tracer study of secondary school leavers in
Malawi can be placed in the context of the total
occupational distribution of the labour force by level of
education. This is shown in table 2.5 for 1977. In that
year, over 70 and 90 percent of male and female primary
school leavers respectively were working as farmers as
were almost .20 percent of secondary school leavers. Taking

Table 2.5. Occupational Breakdown by Level of Education,
            Malawi, 1977 (percent)

	No Education	Primary	Secondary	University
Professional Tech				
Male	0.2	1.3	20.6	53.9
Female	0.1	0.9	36.4	71.9
Managerial				
Male	–	0.1	1.9	13.4
Female	–	–	0.6	4.4
Clerical				
Male	0.2	1.9	23.9	10.6
Female	–	0.3	28.9	14.4
Sales				
Male	2.0	4.3	7.1	4.3
Female	0.6	1.7	6.3	2.6
Service				
Male	2.0	3.7	5.8	0.5
Female	0.5	1.4	3.0	–
Agriculture				
Male	84.8	70.3	18.1	9.4
Female	96.1	92.4	17.1	1.6
Production				
Male	8.1	16.2	18.9	6.0
Female	1.4	2.0	1.9	0.9
Not classified				
Male	2.6	2.3	3.8	1.8
Female	1.2	1.3	5.7	3.6

Source: Government of Malawi (1977).

the first four occupational categories and half the 'production' category as roughly constituting the formal wage earning sector, the percentages of graduates from each educational level employed in this sector were:

	No Education	Primary	Secondary	Higher
Male	10.4	19.3	66.9	82.7
Female	1.9	5.3	75.6	89.4

Since 1977, outputs from the educational system have greatly exceeded the increase in formal sector jobs and the result has, apparently, been an increase in school leaver unemployment. In 1977, primary and secondary school leavers under 24 years experienced urban unemployment rates averaging around 7.5 percent for males and 11.5 percent for females. For the students who sat for junior and middle school certificates in 1976 and whose situations were traced in 1977, 1978 and 1979 unemployment rates were 62, 53 and 50 percent for junior secondary leavers and 35, 16 and 16 percent for middle secondary leavers over the three years. The indication is that the junior secondary leavers are being substituted by those with more schooling and at present they are unwilling to take up employment outside the sector in which their predecessors found jobs. We can surmise that, for this category of school leavers, unemployment rates may grow before they begin to fall.

The activities one year after graduating of secondary forms 3 and 5 leavers in Swaziland in the mid 1970s have also been traced (Sullivan 1981). An interesting aspect of this study was the incorporation of examination performance. Table 2.6 provides the relevant information with Group 1 indicating highest examination achievement, and so on. Proportions in paid employment were similar for both education groups (48 and 43 percent). Proportions unemployed, however, varied considerably (37 percent for form 3 and 22 percent for form 5). The nature of activity being followed one year after graduation also varied by examination performance, with much larger proportions of high achievers following further education and, in the case of form 5, much higher proportions of low achievers being unemployed.

A third tracer study is from Tanzania. The main purpose of this study, conducted over the period 1981-82, was to assess the different educational and labour market performances of secondary school students following pre-vocational and academic streams (Psacharopoulos and Loxley 1985). One year after leaving secondary school form

13

Table 2.6. Activity in First Year After Leaving School by
Level of Education and Examination Group, Swaziland
(percent)

Activity	Form 3				Form 5			
	1	2	3	Total	1	2	3	Total
Further Education	25	19	9	15	72	56	16	35
Paid Employment	41	46	51	48	21	36	52	43
Unemployed	34	35	40	37	7	8	32	22

Source: Sullivan (1981), table 7.

4, only 14.4 percent of graduates were in paid employment
with an additional 7.0 percent searching for employment.
The rest were either in further training or schooling or
looking for places. The very small number of students in
secondary schooling in Tanzania results in favourable
employment prospects or the ability to take up further
education. So far, at least, labour market pressures have
not resulted in significant unemployment nor in the
acceptance of informal sector employment.

In these three countries, secondary school leavers do
not yet appear to be entering the informal sector in large
numbers. Formal sector employment and participation in
further forms of education and training remain the desired
and expected route. The high levels of unemployment one
year after leaving school in Malawi and Swaziland,
however, illustrate the growing difficulties of following
this route.

Some formal sector openings, however, do still exist
and it is important to note how the earnings of those
employed within this sector have been changing over the
last decade or so. Starting salaries in the public service
by education level are shown in index form in table 2.7 for
seven countries around 1979. Apart from Sierra Leone, the
years spent in senior secondary education appear to result
in only small increments in earnings. The addition of
higher education, however, has a substantial effect in four
of the countries, though in three - Ghana, Somalia and
Zambia - the overall differentials are relatively narrow.
More interesting than snapshots at one point in time

Table 2.7 Index of Starting Salaries in Public Service by Education Level

Country	'O' level	'A' level	Degree
Ghana	100	120	169
Kenya	100	127	269
Liberia	100	–	339
Sierra Leone	100	229	342
Somalia	100	128	171
Tanzania	100	148	323
Zambia	100	166	169

Source: Derived from International Labour Office (1982) pp.15-17.

are trends in formal sector earnings differentials. These have recently been compiled for Senegal (Bloch 1985), Zambia (Meesook and Subsaeng 1985), the Sudan (Lindauer and Meesook 1984) and Nigeria (Subsaeng 1984). The data are presented and discussed in detail in chapter 4 but the conclusions can be stated very simply; in each country, for each set of comparisons based on educational or occupational status and in both the private and public sectors earnings differentials in the formal sector have been reduced very substantially over the last decade. In addition, in those countries for which data are available, real earnings of all formal sector employees have fallen. Both the reduced chances of finding formal sector employment and the decreases in earnings differentials which are occurring make it important that the effects of education on those working in the urban informal sector and in agriculture are also analysed.

The Urban Informal Sector. By the nature of the informal sector, data on the characteristics of workers and their conditions of employment are difficult to obtain and have to be collected by special surveys. For African countries these have been relatively few.

15

From a recent survey in Malawi, Etema (1984) presents gross monthly earnings of business owners in the informal sector by level of education. These are (in Kwacha):

No Education	Standard 1-4	Standard 5-8	Post Standard 8
19	29	36	100

Since no additional information on capital use or any other income-related factor is provided, the interpretative use of these figures is limited. They do, however, indicate that differentials by education level exist, and are particularly wide for post primary graduates. Hinchliffe's (1975) study of Nigerian workers also shows positive differentials. In a sample of 397 self employed workers in Kano, 269 had no schooling and 74 had completed primary school. Average annual earnings of these two groups are described in table 2.8. In an earlier study, Hinchliffe (1974) compared incomes in farming, the urban informal sector and in the large textile industry. Due to the almost total lack of schooling among farmers, comparisons were not made by educational level but rather between those with no schooling. Hourly income was calculated at 0.7-1.0 shilling for farming, 1.0 shilling for the urban informal sector and 1.5 shillings for the formal sector. These results tend to confirm that earnings are higher in the formal sector than in the informal sector, although once the comparison is made between similar groups, not by as much as has often been assumed.

The results of a survey of informal sector employment in Banjal, Gambia are also relevant. In 1980, 209 owner/masters were surveyed. While no attempt was made to correlate incomes and education, it was found that certain

Table 2.8. Annual Average Informal Sector Earnings by Age and Schooling, Kano, Nigeria (£)

Schooling	Age Group				
	15-20	21-25	26-30	31-35	36+
None	96	138	145	133	130
Full primary	124	163	127	189	213

Source: Hinchliffe (1975) p. 312.

occupations provided higher incomes than others and that these were dominated by workers with most schooling. It is also interesting to note that in some of these occupations, earnings were higher than the average in the formal sector.

Further evidence on earnings and the educational background of workers in the informal sector comes from Zambia and Ghana. In a study of the informal sector in Lusaka, Todd and Shaw (1979) found that 64 percent of workers had some schooling and that the largest group was those with upper primary. During 1976 to 1980, the National Vocational Training Institute in Ghana reached over 500 rural and urban artisans. Of these, over 80 percent had had a middle school education of ten years (International Labour Office 1982, p.46). Similarly, Aryee's survey of the informal sector in Kumasi in 1975 found that out of 300 owners, 58 percent had middle schooling and of the 20-25 year age group the percentage was just under 80 (Aryee 1976). Middle school education was found to be clearly associated with higher earnings though the effect of primary schooling alone was much weaker.

On the basis of these few studies of the urban informal sector, some conclusions can be reached. First, there now appears to be a readiness to enter the informal sector among primary school leavers and, in countries with relatively well developed education systems such as Ghana, by graduates of junior secondary schools. Second, within the informal sector earnings appear to be positively related to educational level but most obviously for post-primary schooling. Third, while there is some evidence of earnings overlap between individuals in the formal and informal sectors, average earnings by educational level are significantly higher in the formal sector. Overall, both the level of earnings and earnings differentials, at least for primary school leavers, appear to be lower than in the formal sector.

Agriculture. So far, the discussion of the employment effects of education has focussed on the urban sector. The majority of school leavers in African countries, however, work in rural areas as the occupational breakdown for Malawi in table 2.5 showed. Much less is generally known about the effect of education on productivity in this sector and for Africa information is particularly scarce. This discussion begins by summarising the work of Lockheed, Jamison and Lau (1980) which brings together education-farmer productivity studies gathered across developing countries. This is followed by reports of case-studies of farmer education and rural productivity and innovation

17

which have been prepared for African countries.

Lockheed et al. analysed 37 data sets from 18 studies in 13 countries, chiefly of Asia and Latin America, containing data on farmer education and agricultural production. In 31 of the data sets, education was found to have a positive and usually significant effect. The mean annual gain in production for four years of education was 8.7 percent. Following Schultz's (1975) argument that education is likely to be most effective in the context of other 'modernising' conditions the analysis was repeated after dividing the studies according to whether they took place in the context of 'modern' or 'non-modern' conditions. This time, four years of schooling was judged to result in annual increases in output of 1.3 percent in non-modern conditions and 9.5 percent in modern conditions. From these studies, it is clear that while primary schooling may have little payoff in a non-supportive environment, alongside complementary changes the impact of schooling on productivity can be significant.

Few of the studies on farmer education and agricultural outcome which have been made in African countries lent themselves to the form of analysis performed by Lockheed, Jamison and Lau, since most concentrated solely on the adoption of innovations rather than productivity. Of the ten studies collected by Hanson (1981) and reviewed below, only three used measures of productivity. The first of these is by Moock (1973, 1976) who studied the production of maize in Kenya's Western Province and concluded that whereas schooling of between one and three years had no effect on the output of male farmers, increases in output were associated with four years and more of schooling. Each year of schooling was found to result in a 1.7 percent increase in output per year. For female farmers there was a positive association between output and all levels of schooling. Productivity in maize production was also studied by Vanzetti (1972), this time in Zambia. Two communities were surveyed, one with relatively high educational levels and one with low. In the area of high educational levels, farmer productivity was associated with individuals' education. In the area with low educational levels it was not. The impact of education on output was seen to be via motivation rather than farming knowledge and Vanzetti concluded that there is a need for a critical mass of schooled farmers in the community so as to provide mutual reinforcement for the adoption of new practices among them. In the third study focussing on education and productivity Hopcroft (1974), using small farm survey data for Kenya, measured the im-

18

pact of various levels of schooling on the productivity of maize, tea and cattle farming. No association was found.

The remaining studies of the impact of schooling on farming in Africa have concentrated on the adoption of improved practices, rather than directly on productivity. In the first of these Naylor and Ascroft (1966), surveying Kenyan farmers, found that those with some formal schooling were differentiated from the others in various ways, among which were: they knew more about land consolidation, erosion, irrigation and water supplies; they had more money in the bank and sought more loans; they employed more labour and tools and they made more use of extension services. Heyer and Ascroft's (1970) later Kenyan study along similar lines, however, produced far less strong conclusions and high percentages of 'high adopters' were also found among the unschooled. The adoption of innovations in rural development in Meru, Kenya was studied by Almy (1974). Schooling was found to be important, particularly via the development of cognitive skills. A positive effect of schooling on innovation was also found by Heijen (1967) in Mwanza, Tanzania. The suggestion in this study was that schooling plays an important role through creating a receptivity to new ideas and a motivation to implement them. The final East African study, by Moris (1971), produced less positive results. In a survey of Kenyan farmers in Embu District, adult farmers with relatively high levels of schooling were not found to be more innovative than farmers with low or no amounts of schooling.

Turning to West Africa, studies of farmer education and agricultural innovation appear to be even fewer. Rogers, Ascroft and Roling (1970) studied the extent to which villagers adopted innovations promoted by the extension service in 71 Nigerian villages. They also attempted to distinguish 'early and late adopters' and to isolate the determining factors. The conclusion was that schooling's impact was positive. They also supported Vanzetti's argument for Zambia that the educational level of the community is an important factor in stimulating innovation. More recent work on agricultural innovation has been done by Bigelow (1978) in Ghana in four different settings. Fifty farmers were sampled in each and assessed against an innovation index. In no case was farmers' schooling significantly related.

Of these ten studies of schooling and agricultural productivity/innovation in Africa, six suggest that farmers with schooling tend to be more productive and innovative than those without. Where this occurs it appears to result from a mixture of greater motivation, increased cognitive skills and more awareness, and use, of extension agents. Hanson (1981) concludes his survey of these studies by emphasising the point made by both Vanzetti (1972) and Rogers, Ascroft and Roling (1970) that the community's level of education is particularly important,

It would further appear that where attendance at school has become a common pattern, the mutual reinforcement which comes from being with other school leavers with similar motivations encourages a willingness to innovate and to take a chance in the hope of realizing a better future (p.77).

While data on the effect of schooling on productivity in African urban informal and rural sectors remains scarce, that which exists points to a positive relationship. In the formal sector, the relationship is particularly strongly documented. A key question is whether these relationships result directly from education or whether educational level merely identifies those who were more productive to begin with. Hard evidence on this issue is scarce for African countries. However, the results of recent research in Kenya and Tanzania support the argument that educational skills learned do increase productivity (Boissiere, Knight and Sabot 1985). Tests of wage and salaried employees showed that primary school leavers with higher proficiency in literacy and numeracy earn more than secondary leavers with lower proficiency in these areas. In addition, using an ability measure independent of literacy and numeracy skills it was shown that this measure alone has little effect on earnings. Commenting on an earlier report of this study, Bowman and Sabot (1982) conclude 'These findings support the common sense view that literate and numerate workers are more productive and that education is valuable to workers because it gives them skills that increase their productivity' (p.15).

Education, Demographic Change and Health
The economic impact of schooling is not confined solely to behaviour in work. In the last decade or so an increasing amount of attention has been given to examining the relationships, if any, between education and demographic transitions in developing countries resulting, in particular, from changes in fertility and infant and child mortality rates. Studies already show that strong associations exist between education and fertility and mortality rates and between education and the intervening factors. The precise ways in which education influences

these factors, however, still remain largely unclear. Similarly, the economic implications of changing fertility and mortality patterns have hardly begun to be determined but are likely to be substantial as they alter the size and quality of the labour force in a variety of ways. This discussion is divided into two parts. These examine, in turn, the relationships between education and fertility and between education and infant and child mortality.

Education and Fertility. Education provides an individual with a number of attributes: literacy and the access to information, socialisation into different attitudes and behaviour patterns, skills which provide occupational advantages and a certification of status (Cochrane 1979). These affect fertility by increasing knowledge, changing attitudes towards children, altering work patterns and so on and can mostly be expected to reduce levels of fertility.

Analyses of the results of the World Fertility Surveys conducted throughout the developing world have recently been produced by Cochrane and Farid (1984) focussing on the ten sub Saharan African countries included in the Survey, and by Singh, Casterline and Cleland (1985). Levels of fertility are most immediately determined by age of marriage, length of breastfeeding and contraceptive use which in turn are each partially influenced by the socio–economic circumstances of individuals. The relationships between socio–economic circumstances and the proximate determinants of fertility and then of those determinants on fertility levels are the subjects of these analyses.

Levels of fertility in African countries are high relative to all other regions of the world. The reported completed fertility of ever–married women aged 45 to 49 years ranges from 8.3 in Kenya to 5.8 in Lesotho. Of the ten African countries surveyed, fertility trends were downward only in Ghana. This contrasted with falling trends in Asia, Latin America and the Middle East. The immediate causes of high fertility are early and virtually universal marriage and very little use of contraceptive methods. Rates would be even higher were it not for the very high prevalence and long duration of breastfeeding. Each of these factors has been compared across regions with the following results.

- In the African sample, 40 percent of women aged 15–19 years have married compared to 32 percent in the Middle East, 26 percent in Asia and 20 percent in Latin America.
- Contraceptive awareness and use is very low in Africa. Awareness averaged 45 percent compared to

84 percent in Asia and 95 percent in Latin America. Contraceptive use ('ever used'), averaged 26 percent, 40 percent and 61 percent respectively in the three regions. For modern or 'efficient' forms of contraception the averages were 6, 32 and 49 percent.

- Breastfeeding is slightly more prevalent in Africa than in other regions and the average duration of 16–19 months is similar to that recorded in Asia but well above that in Latin America and the Middle East.

The high levels of fertility are not unwanted. For the 15–19 year age group, desired family size in Africa averaged 7.0 compared to 3.3 in Latin America and 3.2 in Asia. In addition, rates of infant and child mortality are highest in Africa.

In the second stage of their analysis, Cochrane and Farid (and also Singh et al.) report differentials in fertility according to various socio-economic factors. Briefly, urban-rural residence has an effect on fertility in Africa but this is lower than in other regions. The effect of husband's occupation produced no generalisations across the ten African countries and neither did mother's work status as measured by wage employment. Turning to mother's education, however, significant differences in fertility were apparent. These are shown below in table 2.9 with equivalent rates for Asia, Latin America and the Middle East. In both the Middle East and Latin America, there is a consistent inverse pattern between education and fertility, while in Africa and Asia fertility increases as the result of a few years of education and declines later. The difference in fertility between those with no education and those with seven or more years is 2.0 in Africa, 2.11 in Asia, 3.43 in Latin America and 4.11 in the Middle East.

The question arises of why the differentials in fertility in Africa are not more affected by education. Several factors lead to an expectation of a more substantial effect:

- differentials in age at marriage by education are larger in Africa than in other regions,
- breastfeeding does not decline among the more educated as in Asia or Latin America,
- differentials in the use of contraceptives by education are greater in Africa.

The answer hinges on the demand for children. There are differentials in the desired family size by level of education in Africa, but at all levels the desired size is greater than in other regions. In other words, at all educational levels women in Africa want more children than

22

Table 2.9. Current Levels of Fertility by Wife's Level of Education

Region	Years of Education			
	None	1-3	4-6	7+
Sub Saharan Africa	6.99	7.43	6.54	4.99
Middle East	8.90	6.91	5.58	4.79
Asia	5.81	5.89	5.66	3.70
Latin America	6.62	6.04	4.71	3.19

Source: Cochrane and Farid (1984), table 8.4.

women elsewhere.   Cochrane and Farid conclude that
compared to other developing regions, 'In general, fertility
in sub Saharan Africa tends to be higher among the rural
and uneducated and fertility falls less with increases in
urban residence and education' (p.80).   However, 'These
data indicate that family size preferences, contraceptive
use and marriage patterns do change with education in
ways which will ultimately lower fertility...' (p.81).

Education and Infant Mortality.   Another aspect of social
behaviour which has been linked to education is infant and
child mortality.   Lower rates of mortality are a benefit to
social welfare in themselves.   They also have economic
returns in terms of extending life expectancy and allowing
greater benefits from early investment in human capital to
be produced. This sub-section begins by summarising the
present state of knowledge regarding the relationship
between parental education and infant and child mortality
and the causal mechanisms involved across developing
countries as a whole.   This is followed by a presentation
of African case studies.

A benchmark study is that by Cochrane, O'Hara and
Leslie (1980) reviewing census and survey tabulations and
household data sets across countries.   On average, an
additional year of mother's schooling was found to be
associated with a 9 per thousand reduction in child
mortality.   Of this, 6 per 1000 were judged to be a direct
result of mother's education and 3 per 1000 a result of a

more schooled woman being married to a more educated, higher income man. Since this review, additional data on infant and child mortality have been collected and analysed for a large number of developing countries through the World Fertility Survey. Using these data, Hobcraft, McDonald and Rutstein (1984) relate under-five mortality and parental education relationships for 28 countries. The results show that on average under-five mortality falls from 152 to 63 per 1000 over the range of mother's education and from 148 to 84 per 1000 over the range of father's education. This corresponds to a fall in child mortality of 9.9 per 1000 for each year of mother's education and 7 per 1000 for father's. Parental education remained significant after controlling for other socio-economic variables. Similarly, the results remain valid after allowing for the negative relationship between parental education and fertility which influences family size and child spacing and hence the survival chances of children. Following these general conclusions based on experiences in developing countries across regions, some studies relating to parental education and child mortality in Africa are now reviewed.

The association between mother's education and infant and child mortality has been well demonstrated in African case-studies: table 2.10 reports findings for ten countries. According to Ware (1984, p.196), studies in other parts of the Third World have shown that the fall in child mortality levels associated with the move from primary to secondary education is twice as important as the original step to primary schooling. On average, this finding also appears to be borne out by the African studies, with mortality rates for children of elementary and post-elementary schooled mothers averaging 28 and 61 percent respectively below those of mothers with no schooling.

Individual case-studies fill out the overall picture of table 2.10. The 1960 census figures for Ghana show the proportion of children dead was almost twice as high for mothers with no education as for those with primary schooling and four times greater than for mothers with secondary schooling (Gaisie 1969). Evidence that mother's education has a direct effect and is not simply a proxy for higher household income comes from Orubuloye and Caldwell (1975) who found that Nigerian women of a similar economic status exhibited wide child mortality differentials by level of education. This occurred in both a community with modern health services and without them. Taking this line of examination further, Caldwell (1979) analysed data on over 8000 Yoruba women in Nigeria to assess the impact of a variety of socio-economic variables on child survival. He

Table 2.10. Proportion of Children Dying by Age X by Mother's Education for Selected African Countries

Country	No School	Elementary	Above Primary
Ethiopia	.179	.137	.012
Gambia	.275	.194	.118
Ghana	.129	.116	.082
Kenya	.160	.106	.043
Senegal[a]	.120	.071	-
Sierra Leone	.292	.217	.140
Sudan (rural)	.212	.151	-
Tanzania	.261	.132	-
Uganda	.181	.129	.056
Zambia[b]	.174	.165	.093

Notes [a]. for Senegal the division is illiterate:literate
      [b]. for Zambia the divisions are no school, lower
           primary, upper primary

Source: Sullivan, Cochrane, Kalsbeek (1982) p.41.

concluded that the single most significant determinant was maternal education and that the other five variables utilised did not together come close to explaining the effect of maternal education. Similar results were found for the Sudan by Farah and Preston (1982).

One determinant of rates of infant and child mortality is nutritional status. The findings of 17 studies relating parental education and child nutritional status have again been reviewed by Cochrane et al. (1980). Of these, five were from Africa including two from South Africa and two from Malawi. Of the twelve studies using years of schooling as the measure of mother's education, seven report a positive and significant relationship. All four studies using female literacy as the measure have positive and significant findings as does the one using education level of the household head.

Documenting the effects of parental education on fertility, child mortality and nutrition is only the first step in determining the economic significance of education in these areas. Fewer children allow parents to 'invest' more in them – more food, more toys, more schooling and so on. In turn this can be expected to increase the cognitive and non-cognitive outcomes resulting from educational expenditures and, later, to increase the economic returns to these expenditures. Hard evidence for these linkages is scarce. While Moock and Leslie (1982) have demonstrated the importance of a child's height-for-age in determining school performance in Nepal and Jamison (1981) has reported similar findings in China, no equivalent studies have been located for African countries. Heyneman and Jamison (1980), however, found a negative relationship in Uganda between indicators of sickness and school achievement.

SUMMARY AND IMPLICATIONS

The suggestion has previously been made that the rate of return evidence available for Africa which shows descending rates for successively higher levels of education may require some qualification. Many of the existing studies are based on earnings data from the 1960s and early 1970s which may not reflect recent changes in earnings structures and which were often collected in ways which led to the urban informal and rural sectors being ignored. There is, then, a strong need for new rate of return studies using age-education-earnings data collected across all economic sectors. In the meantime, two tentative suggestions are made about the way in which the actual pattern of returns to primary and secondary schooling may differ from the recorded ones once allowances are made for trends in formal sector earnings over the past decade and incomes in the informal and rural sectors. First, on the basis of the widely available evidence that very few primary school leavers are now able to find formal sector employment and that the differentials attributable to this level of schooling, while still positive, are lower in the informal and rural sectors than in the formal sector, it is suggested that the returns to primary schooling are lower than the often very high ones recorded. Second, since most secondary school leavers still appear to be able to eventually find formal sector employment in most countries, the earnings differentials between them and primary school leavers may be wider and the rate of return higher than existing studies imply. While no quantitative assessment can be made of these factors here it is suggested that differences in the actual rates of return by level are not as wide as the existing studies suggest and, perhaps more arguably, that it should not be automatically assumed that returns to secondary schooling are below those to primary schooling. Verification must await much needed new rate of return studies covering all sectors of employment.

In the second part of the previous section, attention was given to the effects of education on fertility and child mortality. Several studies, including those based on the recent World Fertility Survey, have demonstrated a negative relationship between a woman's education and the number of children born to her. Variables influencing levels of fertility such as age of marriage, contraceptive use and duration of breastfeeding have similarly each been shown to be significantly related to levels of education. The precise impact of education on fertility, however, and the amount required before there is any impact at all appears to vary between developing regions. At present, the impact is least in sub Saharan Africa and while a completed primary schooling is associated with decreased fertility, those women with just a few years of schooling appear to give birth slightly more often than those with no schooling at all. The major impact of schooling on an African woman's fertility appears to result from secondary schooling.

The amount of parents' education, and particularly the mothers', is also closely related to levels of infant and child mortality across developing countries. This is particularly the case in sub Saharan Africa. The relationship seems to hold strong even after controlling for other socio-economic variables and the influences of family size and child spacing. With regard to the impact of different levels of schooling, the evidence for Africa corresponds with that reported elsewhere - the fall in child mortality associated with the move from primary to secondary education is at least twice as large as that associated with the original step to primary schooling. The latter, however, is also substantial. Turning to the relationship between parental education and child nutritional status there is less evidence for African countries. Evidence from other regions, however, suggests the relationship is strongly positive.

This chapter has attempted to introduce educational development in sub Saharan Africa in a number of ways.

Initially, trends in enrolments and finance were described and attention was drawn briefly to the emphases accorded to the different levels and to their costs. In the second section, some of the economic and social effects of primary and secondary education were described. Not all students terminate their formal education at these levels, however, and a small minority proceed to institutions of higher education. These institutions, and particularly the universities, are the subject of the rest of this book.

3 The development and role of higher education

The first two students to graduate from an African institution of higher education, in the Western tradition, did so in 1879 from Fourah Bay College in Sierra Leone. Not until after the Second World War, however, were additional institutions established and even by 1960 there were only six universities and university colleges in sub Saharan countries. Today with very few exceptions (mainly some of the smaller Portuguese-speaking countries) every sub Saharan African country boasts at least one university. The size of the sector varies considerably between countries. Of the 29 countries with universities affiliated to the Association of African Universities in 1979, 23 had a single university while in Nigeria in the early 1980s there were 20 universities. Enrolments in the universities also vary widely, from around 1000 in those in Burundi, Mozambique, Swaziland, Chad and Niger to over 10,000 in universities in the Ivory Coast, Ethiopia, Nigeria, Sudan, Senegal, Madagascar and Zaire. Enrolments for 50 universities are documented in Appendix Table A3.

The higher education sector in Africa is now widely established but there are several indications that it is not yet secure. Forty years since British and French governments decided to lay the foundations of university education in their African colonies, the role of the universities in these countries is still discussed in books and articles and conflicts between the institutions, their students and governments, continue to be widely reported.

Partly perhaps to justify their cost great claims have been made for the universities, in particular, in sub Saharan Africa which often go well beyond those made for universities in developed countries. All these claims are difficult to fulfil simultaneously and some may even be contradictory. When failure occurs, criticism tends to intensify and resources may be reduced. A vicious cycle is then in danger of being created. These circumstances indicate that a realistic assessment of the potential of the universities in African countries is still required and that while this potential may encompass several dimensions only a very few should be assessed at one time and the constraints appreciated. In the following four chapters, emphasis is placed on the relationship between the universities' output of trained graduates and the labour market, and on the costs of universities and the methods of their financing. In this chapter, some of the current features of the higher education system in sub Saharan Africa are described, together with discussions of the rationale behind the system's growth, its variously perceived role and the suggested shortcomings.

THE HIGHER EDUCATION SECTOR

Enrolments in higher education in sub Saharan Africa increased by an average of around 11 percent a year over the last 25 years. Expansion, however, has been uneven across countries resulting in variations in enrolment ratios (that is, enrolments as a proportion of the 20–24 years old population) ranging between 0.03 percent in Burkina Faso and 7.0 percent in Guinea (see Appendix Table A1). In 1970, higher education enrolments per 100,000 population averaged 53 and by 1980 they had grown to 139. Again, the averages mask wide country variations. In 1980, this ratio was below 50 in 11 countries, between 51 and 100 in 8 countries, between 101 and 200 in 8 countries, between 201 and 300 in 3 countries, and over 300 in 5 countries. The rapid growth in higher education enrolments, however, still places the region as a whole well behind the position of other regions of the world. Enrolments per 100,000 population average around 650 in the Arab and Asian countries and 1250 in Latin America.

The expansion of higher education in African countries has largely been planned on the basis of manpower requirements forecasts and, partly as a corollary, a major emphasis has often been placed on 'vocational' subjects. Table 3.1 shows the division of enrolments in 1980 for Western and Eastern Africa country groups between Arts, Social and Business Studies, and Science and Vocational Studies. In both sets of countries, but particularly in Eastern Africa, the science and vocational subjects have clearly received highest priority.

Despite the high rates of growth of enrolments in higher education, as a proportion of all enrolments they remain less than one percent across the region as a whole. This contrasts strongly to the sector's share of the total education budget which averages around 19 percent. Table 2.3 gave examples of the distribution of expenditure between education levels and changes in that distribution

Table 3.1. Distribution of Higher Education Enrolment by
            Field of Study, 1980 or nearest

Region	Arts	Social Studies	Science and Vocational
Western Africa	32	33	35
Eastern Africa	27	28	45
Sub Saharan Africa	30	31	40

Source: UNESCO (1983).

over time. In all cases, the proportion allocated to higher
education had been increasing. In table 3.2, countries are
categorised according to the current share of recurrent
educational expenditure allocated to higher education. The
range is very wide. Lowest shares are for Mauritius,
Zimbabwe, Benin, Niger and Gambia (7 percent and under)
and highest for Upper Volta, Burundi, Guinea, Lesotho,
Malawi, Zaire and Mauritania (25 percent and over).

Table 3.2. Distribution of sub Saharan African Countries
            by Share of Total Education Expenditure
            for Higher Education

| | Percent of Total Recurrent Expenditure on Higher Education | | | |
	0-10	11-20	21-30	31+
Number of Countries	8	13	10	1

Source: World Bank (1985).

     High shares of educational expenditure relative to
enrolments suggest that the unit costs of higher education
are large in relation to those for other levels of education.
In many African countries they are also large in absolute
terms compared to countries in most other regions of the
world. Further, since per capita incomes in the region are

mainly among the lowest in the world, the cost of a higher education in Africa is particularly high relative to overall domestic resources. These points are illustrated comprehensively country-by-country in chapter 6. In table 3.3 below, some of the relevant summary statistics are presented.

Table 3.3.   Unit Costs of Public Education by Level as a Percentage of Per Capita Gross National Product

Region/Country Group	Primary	Secondary	Higher
Sub Saharan Africa			
Francophone	29	143	804
Anglophone	18	50	920
Asia			
South East Asia & Pacific	11	20	118
South Asia	8	18	119
Latin America	9	26	88
All Developing Countries	14	41	370

Source: Mingat and Psacharapoulos (1984) p.12.

As a final introductory comment on the scale of the higher education sector in sub Saharan Africa, it is important to mention the place of overseas study. Before 1960, the majority of African university graduates had been trained overseas. For instance, in Nigeria in 1960, 182 students graduated from the University College of Ibadan while around four times that number graduated from overseas institutions. The rapid growth of higher education in Africa has not led to any absolute reduction in overseas students. In fact between 1972 and 1980, the numbers increased from 59,000 to 178,000. Moock (1984) argues that these now represent 30 percent of all African students enrolled at the tertiary level. Table 3.4 shows the growth in overseas enrolments for selected African countries. The bias towards professional, scientific and technological studies in local universities shown in table 3.1 is also reflected, at an even greater intensity, in the placing of students abroad. For example, British Council

Table 3.4. African Students Studying Abroad in 45 Selected
Countries, 1972, 1980

Country of Origin	Overseas Enrolments	
	1972	1980
Botswana	41	355
Ghana	1912	3158
Ivory Coast	919	3648
Nigeria	6289	26,863
Senegal	569	2848
Cameroon	1173	5288
Zambia	306	1039

Source: UNESCO (1974, and 1983).

statistics on overseas students for 1977/78 show almost three quarters enrolled in these fields (Oxenham 1981, p.154). In the United States, African students are enrolled across subjects in the following proportions: engineering 20 percent, business studies 19 percent, social science 12 percent and natural sciences 9 percent (Moock 1984, p.229).

The very bare, aggregate figures and descriptions provided in this section are filled out somewhat in Appendix B where short accounts of the higher education sector in 23 countries are provided. These accounts vary substantially in terms of coverage and the date of the information. Despite this variability, two main features emerge. First, apart from Nigeria where university enrolments alone were over 100,000 in 1985, the absolute numbers of students are very low. In 13 of the 23 countries they are below 4500. Second, despite the average percentage of students enrolled in science and vocational studies being 40 percent according to UNESCO figures presented in table 3.1, in several individual countries the percentages are very low. Examples are: Benin 20 percent, Botswana 22 percent, Burundi 15 percent, Cameroon 18 percent, Senegal 10 percent and Togo 20 percent. At the same time there is a widely expressed determination, often

33

expressed in targets, to increase the proportions of enrolments in science, engineering and professional studies. However, as will be shown later in this book, these subjects are often much more expensive to provide and the inadequacy of secondary schooling in maths and science often results in even existing places not being filled.

THE ROLE OF THE UNIVERSITIES

Although the majority of Africa's universities were established in the 1960s a few institutions (in addition to Fourah Bay) have now been in existence as fully-fledged university colleges or universities for almost 40 years. Further, post secondary education below degree level was first offered at Makerere College, Uganda in 1922, Gordon Memorial College and the Kitchener School of Medicine, in the Sudan in 1924, Achimota College in the Gold Coast in 1927 and Yaba College in Nigeria in 1933.

For the British government the first step in the establishment of African universities was the 1933 Report of the Advisory Committee on Education, devoted to higher education in the colonies. The Report had little immediate impact, though in 1940 Makerere College became a College of Higher Education. Other African countries had to await the findings of the Asquith Committee in 1945 and the subsequent founding in 1948 of university colleges in the Sudan, Nigeria and the Gold Coast, each having a 'special relationship' with London University. Additional university colleges with a similar arrangement were later established in Tanzania, Kenya and Southern Rhodesia. Almost immediately upon independence each of these colleges became fully-fledged universities. In the same way that institutions of higher education in English speaking colonies were linked to the University of London and had degree standards guaranteed by that university, so the universities of Dakar and Abidjan (and later, other universities in French-speaking countries) were linked to Paris and Bordeaux while the University of Leopoldville was linked to the University of Louvain (Wandira 1977, p.42). In French-speaking countries, the 'special relationships' survived independence with Dakar University requesting adoption as France's eighteenth university while all degrees continued to be issued by the French Ministry of National Education until 1968 (Ki-Zerbo 1973, p.21.).

These formal links between old, established European universities and the fledgling African ones not surprisingly led to attempted imitation at all levels by the new universities and, at least initially, to a similarity of per-

34

ceived roles. According to Ashby (1964), the basic assumption of the Asquith 'doctrine' was that the colonial universities' primary purpose was to '...produce men and women with standards and capacity for leadership which self rule requires'. Commenting with respect to Nigeria, Austin (1980) describes how this was seen to require

> ...a university on the gold standard, presented with the seal of international approval and charged with high ideals. It was intended to educate a locally rooted, nationally minded elite able to unite the young federation as civil servants and professional men and women, while upholding academic standards as members of a wider universe of learning (p.207).

The university colleges were to nurture and sustain an intellectual elite through the same organisation, procedures and virtually the same curriculum as English universities. Except for a few critics, who in most cases had been educated outside both Africa and Britain, this view was not controversial at the time, '...initially there was no problem of adaptation. The African wanted a replica of the British university at its best; the expatriate staff had no other model to offer' (Ashby, 1964, p.22).

The demand by Africans that their universities mirror those in the metropolitan countries as a way of ensuring equal standards has gradually evolved over the past 30 years. This has occurred partly as a result of a growing confidence within the institutions but mainly as a response to social and political forces outside. Essentially, the demand for change has been made in two separate but overlapping areas. First, there has been the call for Africanisation of the universities, most importantly in curricula. Second, there have been pressures for the purposes and functions of the universities to be perceived differently from those in Europe. It is this second aspect which is of concern here.

That a single, national university in a recently independent country will have a different relationship to the society of which it is a part than will a well established university which is one of many in a society which has witnessed a confident political and cultural continuity for centuries is readily accepted (Wandira 1977). Ashby (1964) describes the differences in the following way, '...the social purpose of a university in Africa differs from its traditional social purpose in Europe. In Europe, universities have stood for continuity and conservation; in Africa universities are powerful instruments for change' (p.98). The issue is how that power can be maximised. Disagreement occurs between those who measure the universities' effectiveness by the amount of its direct involvement in the wider community and those who argue that effectiveness is exercised most efficiently indirectly through well educated students and a detached focus on learning and the creation of knowledge.

During the 1960s and 1970s the community role of the universities was probably expressed most often and by both African politicians and academics. Presidents Nkrumah and Nyerere provide examples of the former: 'While I fully subscribe to the vital principle of academic freedom, a university must relate its activities to the needs of the society in which it exists...' (Nkrumah 1964) and 'Even if it were desirable, we are too poor in money and educated manpower to support an ivory tower existence for an intellectual elite...We must, and do, demand this university take an active part in the social revolution we are engineering (Nyerere 1964)'. Almost a decade after these speeches were made, the question of the role of African universities was still being debated and a workshop was held under the auspices of the Association of African Universities to 'formulate a new philosophy of higher, particularly university, education for Africa' (Yesufu 1973, p.5).

At the workshop, the traditional view of the university was put by Ajayi (1973, p.11) – a group of scholars and students living together as a community and claiming a large measure of autonomy – and was rejected as inadequate. The roles which the workshop decided were appropriate for the truly African university were very different and seemingly more ambitious. These were:
a) Pursuit, promotion and dissemination of knowledge: with an emphasis on practical knowledge, locally oriented.
b) Research: with an emphasis on research into local problems affecting the immediate community.
c) Provision of intellectual leadership: not only the production of knowledge but also its wide diffusion for meaningful programmes of economic and social development.
d) Manpower development: including the participation in training middle level manpower and the shift in degree programmes away from the purely academic to the practical and professional.
e) Promoting social and economic modernisation: through example and activities outside the university including extension work with small scale traders, artisans and farmers.
f) Promoting intercontinental unity and international un-

36

derstanding: through providing the foundation to reinforce the positive image of Africa.

More recent expression of these ideas can be found in the National Policy Paper on Education published by the Nigerian Ministry of Education in 1978. This exhorted the universities to provide high level manpower within the needs of the economy, inculcate a proper value-orientation for the individual and society, use the talents and expertise in the universities more for national development and decisionmaking than at present, encourage a spirit of service in the students and serve as effective instruments for cementing national unity. These functions go well beyond those claimed for, or expected from, traditional European universities.

The 'ideal type' of university evolving from such expanded sets of functions has been termed by Lauglo (1982) as utilitarian. Its main purpose is to serve the development needs of society as formulated by political authorities by structuring its size and programmes to manpower forecasts and its curriculum to immediate social and economic problems. The implications, however, go further since what is being called for is a substantial and direct involvement of the university in the immediate concerns of the community. Attempts to put this wider concept of the role of universities into practice have been numerous and examples from Ethiopia, Cameroon, Ghana, Mali, Nigeria, Tanzania and elsewhere are documented in Thompson and Fogel (1976). Most have involved the creation of departments or units expressly designed to work with groups outside the university, or on activities which take students and faculty into rural areas.

Two forms of criticism have been levelled at the attempts by universities to significantly increase their direct involvement in the community. Williams (1981) argues that in certain cases activities such as '...graduates in the fields capturing colorado beetles, or helping nomads to make audio visual aids in a rural community improvement centre...' (p.22) represent nothing more than universities playing at development through expensive gestures and engaging in window dressing to impress governments or aid agencies. More important is the argument that such projects are an inefficient use of university resources and that the pressures on universities to expand their roles in the directions described are extremely detrimental to their main role of providing high quality teaching. This view has been forcefully put forward by Shils (1981),

One of the main problems is that so much is expected of

universities in poor countries. Some of these
expectations are unreasonable, requiring of universities
what no university could deliver yet diverting them from
what they could do (p.45).

A similar view is held by Wandira (1977). There is no
disagreement, he argues, as to the ways in which
universities could serve communities. The question is
whether small and young universities are capable and have
the resources to follow these ways. If not, the failed
attempts will lead to a dangerous disillusionment. While
the objectives of expanded roles may be generally
acceptable, the reality of funding imposes its own
constraints.

Thus the poorest countries of Africa find that they cannot
afford the university they need for their development. In
turn, poor universities are unable to make as significant
a contribution to the development of their countries as
they would like (p.54).

With limited resources choices must be made. That choice
is not necessarily between a 'relevant' university and one
totally divorced from the surrounding society. Relevance
can mean the equipping of graduates to perform effectively
in post-university life. It does not necessitate the
university's involvement in extension programmes to small
traders and artisans.
    The general issue of the appropriate functions and
orientation of universities in poor countries has produced a
great deal of rhetoric and breast beating. Each position
can be hidden behind by basically unsuccessful
institutions. Perhaps a more important question at this
time is how well do the universities perform the functions
they do adopt? For an intellectually sterile university to
take a stand against greater community involvement would
result in the worst of all worlds. Similarly, a university
which poured resources into unsuccessful outreach
programmes to the detriment of its internal teaching
programme would again serve no-one's purpose. The
central problem for the universities, as Lauglo (1982)
argues, is how to improve the quality of academic work.
This may be stimulated or perverted by pressures for
active community involvement.
    Universities are expensive and there is an
expectation that the benefits from the output will be more
than equal to the costs. Whatever the orientation, the
teaching function of African universities is likely to remain
paramount and graduates will be the most important out-

put. This output then needs evaluating. One form of evaluation is to compare the academic quality of graduates from one university with a general standard. External examiners and, sometimes, accreditation arrangements exist for such purposes. Another form is to use the assessment of the labour market. In the remainder of this book, the evaluation of universities largely concentrates on this latter form of assessment.

PLANNING CRITERIA IN HIGHER EDUCATION

The establishment and development of the higher education sector in sub Saharan Africa has been shown to have been based on several rationales. The major one, however, has been to produce highly trained manpower capable of replacing expatriates and to be available for the new demands generated by expected high rates of economic growth. The scope for replacing expatriates in the 1960s can be seen from table 3.5 which shows, for eleven African countries, expatriate employment as a proportion of total employment in four skill categories. On average expatriates filled over 60 percent of jobs requiring a post secondary education.

The desire for a rapid growth in enrolments led to the search for a planning methodology and that adopted has had a significant impact on the evolution of African countries' higher education systems. The initial expansion of higher education occurred at a time when economic policymaking had embraced the concept of 'comprehensive development planning' and the ability of planning authorities to not only forecast but also guide the development of the economy was taken for granted. Most planning models assumed strong, simple relationships between inputs and outputs, for example between investment and gross national product. In this context, the common approach taken to educational planning was based on similar perceptions and followed similar approaches. From a forecast rate of economic growth, the manpower requirements necessary to support that growth were calculated on the assumption of direct relationships between output and different types of manpower. These manpower requirements were in turn transformed into education equivalents. Over the last 25 years, the precise methodologies used have grown more sophisticated but continue to be based on the same basic assumptions. As an example, the experiences in Nigeria of formulating higher education policy are informative.

Medium term planning of higher education in Nigeria began in 1960 with the publication of the Ashby Commission

Table 3.5. Expatriate Employment as a Percentage of Total Employment at Different Levels of Skilled and Educated Manpower

Country	Year of Survey	Educational Level				Total
		A	B	C	D	
Botswana	1967	94		81	19	42
Ivory Coast	1962	79	61			
Kenya	1964	77	25	54	18	48
	1969	58	48	36		41
Malawi	1966	64	10	14		18
Nigeria	1964	39	5			13
Somalia	1970	7	2	20	2	2
Sudan	1967–68	12	6	2	0	3
Swaziland	1970	80	74	57	23	35
Tanzania	1965	82	23	31	9	31
	1969	66	20	12	6	18
Uganda	1967	66	32	16	11	21
Zambia	1965–66	96	92	88	41	62

Notes: A = university degree or equivalent

B = A levels or O levels plus formal training

C = O levels or secondary form 2 plus formal training

D = secondary form 2 or primary plus formal training

Source: Jolly and Colclough (1972).

report, the terms of reference for which were 'to conduct an investigation into Nigeria's needs in the fields of Post Secondary and Higher Education over the next twenty years' (Federal Republic of Nigeria 1960, p.2.). The general approach of the Commission was indicative of the prevailing attitude at the time,

> We could have approached this task by calculating what the country can afford to spend on education and by proposing cautious, modest and reasonable ways in which the education system might be improved within the limits of our budget. We have unanimously rejected this approach to our task (p.4).

The implication was that the educational system had to expand at any cost.

The Commission's recommendations for expansion were based solely on manpower requirements estimates provided by Harbison for 1960 to 1970. These estimates were divided into two categories, Senior manpower requiring a university degree and Intermediate manpower requiring two or three years post secondary education, and were said to be based on considerations of stocks and existing vacancies, interviews with officials and personal judgements. Assuming a 4 percent rate of economic growth, the target annual rates of growth for Senior and Intermediate level manpower were 8 and 13 percent respectively. On the basis of these manpower targets, the Ashby Commission drew up educational targets for 1970. After modification by the Federal Government, these were used as a basis for educational expansion in the National Development Plan 1962–68. Between 1960 and 1962, the number of universities increased from one to five.

The influence of the Harbison–Ashby approach in Nigeria also extended to later in the decade. A first major attempt to survey high level manpower and forecast future requirements in detail was made in 1964. At a seminar held to discuss the forecasts made by the National Manpower Board it was recommended that the experience of other developing countries had shown that the growth in the level of employment was approximately equal to half of the growth rate of national income; and the rates of growth of demand for Senior and Intermediate personnel were generally two and three times the rate of growth of national income respectively. (Very similar to the target rates of growth adopted by the Ashby Commission!) These recommendations were then accepted.

In the Second National Development Plan 1970–74, the government adopted a more complex manpower forecasting methodology based on that developed by Parnes for the Mediterranean Regional Project (Parnes 1962). First, sectoral output estimates for the Plan period were used to estimate employment, assuming no changes in the pre-Plan relationships between trends in employment and output. To these sectoral employment estimates, occupational mixes taken from a 1965 survey were applied to derive occupational totals which were then summed over all sectors. The inadequate statistical base for this exercise was admitted, 'The procedures adopted were in certain respects determined primarily by the fact that time and data were not available for making alternative estimates' (Federal Republic of Nigeria 1970, p.329).

The major expansion of higher education in Nigeria, however, resulted from the Third Plan 1975-80 in which high level manpower was listed as one of the seven principal objectives. Again, forecasts were made on the basis of the Parnes methodology and high levels of shortages were anticipated. During this period, the number of universities increased from 6 to 13 and enrolments from 32,000 to 58,000. In 1977, a major manpower survey was made which formed the basis of occupational requirement forecasts in the Fourth Plan 1981-85. These forecasts were in certain cases built up from individual projects and were extremely detailed. Massive shortages were again identified, often equal to existing stocks; and once again large increases in enrolments in the universities and polytechnics were planned – from 67,000 to 109,000 for the universities and from 41,000 to 70,000 for the polytechnics. Considering the influence which the manpower forecasts have had for 20 years on plans for the development of higher education in Nigeria it is salutory to note the comments in the Fourth Plan on their reliability,

The recent improvements in our data base ... cannot be regarded as adequate, since other important manpower data are not yet available. The absence of these, together with the deficiences in the available data, have continued to militate against the reliability of our forecasts (p.444).

This is not the place for an extensive critique of the Harbison approach which dominated educational planning in the early 1960s, not only in Nigeria, but also in East Africa and South East Asia. Critiques of this approach and of the more sophisticated manpower forecasting methodology developed by Parnes already exist (Blaug 1970, Hinchliffe 1985, Psacharopoulos and Woodhall 1985). Of relevance to the arguments developed in this book, however, two points can be made. First, while the establishment of universities in Africa may have resulted from a range of motivations stemming from a rather broad conceptualisation of their purposes and benefits, the size and composition of the sector has been dominated by considerations of manpower development. The second point is that the methodology overwhelmingly adopted for this purpose includes no consideration of costs. University graduates are seen to be needed or required according to forecasts of economic growth and the manpower forecasting approach contains no disciplinary element in terms of the costs of providing them. This lack of financial discipline initially had important effects on the way in which the first batch of African universities, in particular, was built and operated. The design of these universities, in turn, strongly influenced those which have been established since. The financial implications are discussed in detail in chapter 6, but in the final section of this chapter, a brief description is given of the several forms of criticism currently being levelled at the higher education sector.

CURRENT CRITICISMS OF THE HIGHER EDUCATION SECTOR

For a variety of reasons, the higher education sector today is on the defensive in African countries as in many other developing countries. The critique is based on a number of fronts, some of which can be inferred from earlier parts of this chapter. Here, the critiques are presented and some initial comments are made. No conclusions are drawn, however, until further discussion in the following chapters.

While there has been a virtual consensus that the primary purpose of universities and other institutions of higher education is to produce qualified manpower, previous discussion has shown that this has not meant that there have been no debates over the form and place of higher education in developing countries. These debates have focussed on curricula, academic freedom and the general relationship between the institutions and society at large. Criticisms have been made that higher education institutions are elitist, isolated, further the attitude of self importance among students rather than fostering ideals of community service, encourage the transfer of Western ideology, reinforce the emerging patterns of status stratification and altogether operate as imported institutions. These issues are not discussed further in this book.

A second set of criticisms is based on the impact which higher education is said to have on the rest of the educational system. It has been argued that the emphasis on examination success for entering the sector (together with the overuse of qualifications in the labour market) distorts and narrows what is taught and learned in secondary schools. In particular, it is said that there is a downgrading of 'non-academic' skills which are of importance to the majority of secondary school leavers who must immediately enter the labour market. The same processes also extend down to the primary school. This suggested distortion of the whole education system by the values of the higher education sector is said to be much greater in the developing countries in which formal schooling is virtually the only vehicle for career advancement and where earnings differentials are very much wider than in the industrialised countries. Again, no empirical data are presented in the rest of this book to counter or support these claims of distortion.

A third area in which criticism is directed towards the higher education sector is in its so-called 'external efficiency' - that is, the degree to which its outputs (in the rest of this book defined as graduates and research) correspond to societies' demands and are of value in relation to their costs of production. In terms of the education and training of students, the critique comes in two forms:

- that the scale and/or structure of the sector has resulted in the persistence of shortages in some manpower fields and in surpluses trained in fields of low priority;
- that the overall rates of return to investment in higher education are lower than in several other sectors and in particular are low in relation to other education levels - also that returns vary substantially by subject, again reflecting an inappropriate structure of expansion.

These critiques are documented and judged in chapter 4 according to the evidence available for African countries.

The final set of criticisms revolves around the concept of internal efficiency, or the efficiency with which the sector uses resources to produce educated and trained graduates. The starting point for such criticisms is the high unit costs of higher education borne by African states in relation to other levels of education, levels of income in the countries concerned and costs in other regions of the world. High unit costs have a number of causes including teaching salaries far above per capita income, low student/ teaching staff ratios resulting in part from a proliferation of specialist courses, large numbers of non-teaching staff, subsidised staff housing and free student accommodation. Added to these high unit costs, in several African countries substantial scholarships and living allowances are paid to students. Some of the relevant data were produced earlier in this chapter. Much more is presented in chapters 6 and 7 and in the case studies in chapter 8.

4 The graduate labour market

There are two concepts of efficiency applicable to analysis of the higher education sector – internal and external efficiency. Internal efficiency focusses on the amount and utilisation of resources used to produce the sector's output. In chapter 3 it was shown that the presumed outputs of the higher education sector are numerous, ranging from the graduation of students to the maintenance of national culture. For simplicity, in the rest of this book outputs are taken to be of two types – graduating students and research. In economic analysis, cost effectiveness assessments provide measures of internal efficiency. In practice, analyses of internal efficiency in higher education use such indicators as repetition rates, dropout rates, class sizes, teacher contact hours, intensity of use of facilities and overall unit costs. These are discussed for the higher education sector in sub Saharan Africa in chapter 6. The external efficiency of higher education institutions is concerned with the impact of their operations on the economy and society as a whole. In economic theory, the appropriate instrument to measure this efficiency is cost benefit analysis. However, as is discussed below, some suspicion of this approach as applied to education exists and in practice analyses have also concentrated on levels of unemployment, manpower shortages, the quality and effectiveness of graduates in work, the amount of research and its relevance to national needs, and other such indicators. The external efficiency of the higher education sector in sub Saharan Africa is the subject of this chapter.

The chapter begins with a presentation of the standard argument that higher education in developing countries has been overexpanded either in general or in specific subjects leading to widespread unemployment or severe imbalances in the markets for high level manpower. Methods of testing this proposition are discussed in general terms and then its applicability to African countries is focussed on. A start is made with the presentation of rate of return studies followed by a discussion of wage trends.

This is then augmented by country descriptions which utilise a range of indicators including levels of expatriate employment, public service vacancies, tracer studies and manpower forecasts. In the final two sections, suggestions are made concerning the more efficient working of the graduate labour market and, very briefly, the place of research in higher education institutions.

THE LABOUR MARKET FOR HIGHER EDUCATION GRADUATES

There is a conventional wisdom in general discussions of developing countries that unemployment among higher education graduates and/or a mal-utilisation of graduates widely exists alongside continuing shortages in particular science-based occupations. The empirical evidence for this view has often been taken from Asian countries but the 'dangers' of school leaver and eventually higher education surpluses, have also been pointed to in discussions of African countries for several years. In chapter 3, a brief description of this generalised view was presented in two forms. Below, a similar view is reproduced from the Economic Commission for Africa (1978):

> Firstly there is evidence of growing open unemployment of secondary and even tertiary school leavers in African countries. Secondly, the forecasts of manpower requirements in African countries in recent years are increasingly yielding predictions of middle level and higher level manpower surpluses...Thirdly, there is evidence that the social rate of return on investment in education is higher in primary education than in any other level of education...by and large in the continent as a whole it is true to say that all the indicators point toward a possible overexpansion of the upper levels of the educational system (pp.85-6).

In much of the rest of this chapter these arguments are developed further and the evidence surveyed. A start is made by considering some of the problems involved in measuring the degree of labour market imbalance.

Measures and Causes of Labour Imbalance

Identifying shortages and surpluses of specific manpower categories is not simple. The most common approach has been to concentrate on the level of unfilled vacancies and for relatively highly educated people in most African countries, this mainly involves vacancies in the public sector. For teachers, doctors, extension workers and the like, establishments are determined according to

46

size of service population and norms of service, such as teacher:pupil ratios. Such norms always involve a large degree of subjectivity and arbitrariness. This is even more so in the case of central and local government administrators. How many trained economists does a ministry of finance actually need? Turning to sectors producing for the markets, vacancies again are not unambiguous. In parastatal enterprises not directly operated on rigorous efficiency criteria, establishments may again be created for many reasons other than that the value of increased output would match or exceed the additional wage bill. The same is true for the monopolistic sections of the private sector.

While the presence of vacancies does not necessarily constitute a true shortage, the employment of expatriates can be used as an indicator of at least minimum levels. Although there are almost always possibilities for reorganising work patterns and combinations of workers with various skills, the retention of expatriates on often high wages is a reasonable indication of unmet demand. Another indicator of manpower shortages may be escalating wage rates as employers compete for inadequate supplies of particular skills. However, while their presence may indicate shortages, an absence of rising rates is not conclusive evidence that shortages do not exist. Government control of wages may rule these out and a much more careful analysis of job grading may be required.

Turning to indicators of labour surpluses, the most common approach is to measure open unemployment and the time taken to find first employment. Whether unemployment and long periods of job search are truly indicative of surpluses depends partly on their causes. These could include, an unambiguous lack of jobs of the type to utilise the skill learned and at a wage similar to that in the immediate past, a poorly functioning labour market in which information on vacancies is only slowly transmitted, or a labour market in which wide wage differentials exist between jobs such that it is in the individual's interest to wait for a long period of time until a high paying job becomes available. Another major problem in using unemployment measures as the indicator of surpluses is that in countries such as Ethiopia, Guinea, Mali and Somalia, employment for graduates is guaranteed by the government in which case no visible surpluses are allowed to exist. One other measure of surplus is low or falling wage rates. Again, however, only if the market is being allowed to set these rates can they operate as a useful indicator.

The employment indicators described above can provide some, partial, information on the current state of, and trends in, the graduate labour market and whether there has been over- or under-expansion of higher education in terms of jobs. If wage rates are used, this also tells us something about demand, in an economic sense. All this information, however, is insufficient for assessing whether the resources allocated to higher education are being used efficiently. For instance, shortages as indicated by large numbers of vacancies may exist and many expatriates may be employed in a situation where the costs of training appropriate labour would be much greater than the increases in output produced by that labour. On the other hand, open unemployment rates may be relatively high and periods required to gain employment lengthy yet the additional output produced by graduates when they do find work could have a far greater value than the costs involved in producing them. If then the concern is with the appropriate level of resources being directed towards higher education and the efficient allocation of this within the sector, measures of social rates of return become, in principle, relevant. Rates of return to investment in higher education need to be compared to those of investments at other levels if the concern is with efficient allocation within the education sector as a whole, and returns by separate higher education area are required if the concern is with efficiency within the higher education sector alone.

Why might imbalances in skills produced within the higher education sector and identified by either differences in unemployment rates, periods of job search and/or wage rates or by significant differences in rates of return, exist? There are three major reasons – inadequate information about future labour market conditions available to both students and those responsible for providing higher education places, an insufficient number of qualified school leavers available or willing to take up places offered and institutional rigidities that hinder rapid labour supply adjustments. These are briefly looked at in turn.

Higher education is characterised by long gestation periods. As a consequence, labour market conditions at the time of graduation may differ substantially from those existing at the time when individuals made their course decisions and when the authorities decided on the number and distribution of places. One possible result is that markets for educated labour are subject to cycles of under- then over-supply. The long gestation period is also a feature used to justify basing the provision of higher education places on manpower forecasts. Unfortunately, the experiences with these forecasts have in general not proved satisfactory in developing countries. Economic growth and structural changes have varied widely from those forecast, productivity and skill mixes have departed from the assumptions, and skills have been formed in ways other than those anticipated. Even if the future behaviour of labour markets was identified accurately by students and policymakers, there is no guarantee that places provided on this basis would be taken up. On the one hand students' career choices may be made on grounds other than the purely economic. On the other, there may be a lack of students qualified in subjects required as a basis for advanced courses. Finally, even if changes in labour demand were accurately forecast by both students and education planners and even if students were qualified and willing to adjust their choices accordingly, there is no guarantee that higher education institutions would make the necessary adjustments to their programmes. Faculty tenure, elaborate decisionmaking procedures and the semi-autonomous status of many higher education institutions make rapid change unlikely. Added to this, those fields where there are labour shortages and where expansion is desirable are precisely the ones for which higher education teachers are likely to be most scarce.

Labour market imbalance in terms of either a general surplus of graduates or a mixture of shortages and surpluses seems to be a common assumption for African countries. The data required to fully test this assumption, however, are not available for any of these countries. In the analysis which follows the state of the current, and likely future, labour market for higher education graduates in sub Saharan Africa is reviewed using a battery of, admittedly, partial evidence.

Rates of Return

Calculations of rates of return to investment in education were mentioned briefly in chapter 2 and some scepticism about the ability of existing studies to reflect the current state of labour markets in Africa was shown. That discussion is now extended. Returns have been calculated for at least 15 sub Saharan countries and the results are shown in table 4.1.

Across all countries, the average returns are:

	Primary	Secondary	Higher
Private	45	24	32
Social	27	17	12

Before aspects of the methodology behind these calculations and the use which can be made of them are discussed, the

Table 4.1. The Returns to Investment in Education by Level, Africa (percent)

Country	Year	Social Primary	Social Secondary	Social Higher	Private Primary	Private Secondary	Private Higher
Botswana	1983	42.0	41.0	15.0	99.0	76.0	38.0
Ethiopia	1972	20.3	18.7	9.7	35.0	22.8	27.4
Ghana	1967	18.0	13.0	16.5	24.5	17.0	37.0
Kenya	1971	21.7	19.2	8.8	28.0	33.0	31.0
	1980		13.0			14.5	
Lesotho	1980	10.7	18.6	10.2	15.5	26.7	36.5
Liberia	1983	41.0	17.0	8.0	99.0	20.5	17.0
Malawi	1978		15.1				
Nigeria	1982	14.7	15.2	11.5	15.7	16.8	46.6
Rhodesia	1966	23.0	12.8	17.0	30.0	14.0	34.0
	1960	12.4					
Sierra Leone	1971	20.0	22.0	9.5			
Somalia	1983	20.6	10.4	19.9	59.9	13.0	33.2
Sudan	1974		8.0	4.0		13.0	15.0
Tanzania	1982		5.0				
Uganda	1965	66.0	28.6	12.0			
Upper Volta	1970	25.9	60.6				
	1975	27.7	30.1	22.0			
	1982	20.1	14.9	21.3			

Source: Psacharopoulos (1985) Appendix Table A-1.

implications of the results will be briefly set out. The social returns are highest for primary schooling in eight of the twelve countries for which there are full sets of returns. In ten out of 14 cases, returns to higher education are lowest and are below 10 percent in five cases. The implications of these results are that within the education budget existing resources, at least for the time being, and any increases, should be switched away from higher education towards the other levels. The appropriate overall level of resources for the education sector, of course, depends on a comparison with returns in the other sectors.

The apparent simplicity and the strong implications of these social rates of return require that the methodology followed in their calculation be looked at carefully. Leaving aside the fundamental questions of the meaning of the relationships between earnings and marginal productivity (particularly in the public sector) and productivity and education, the earnings data used should utilise realistic assessments of lifetime differentials. Since it has not proved possible to accurately forecast changes in the earnings differentials through time the standard methodology has been to use cross sectional data on the assumption that age-education-earnings differentials will remain similar to those observable today. In inspecting rate of return studies, therefore, the best form of earnings data that can be hoped for is cross sectional data based either on the population census or on large, well constructed sample surveys.

In only three of the twelve African case studies for which there are complete sets of returns are cross sectional data based on sample surveys used and most of the rest are based directly on civil service pay scales. All but one of those studies which are based on sample surveys are limited to the urban sector.

Another data problem relates to costs. In all the studies the costs of producing graduating students have been inflated through the attribution of all institutional costs to this purpose. To the extent that there are outputs other than graduates, the teaching costs should be reduced with a consequent increase in the rates of return.

A final point to be considered in surveying these studies of returns to higher education is that just over half were based on data from the 1960s and early 1970s. Since then enrolments have increased by an average of 11 percent a year, public sector employment has exploded and expatriates have been widely replaced. It cannot be simply assumed, therefore, that the separate forces acting on the demand and supply for higher education graduates have operated in such a way that returns have remained constant.

Social rates of return to investment in education can be powerful tools of analysis if the earnings data used can be assumed to reasonably reflect different levels of productivity between graduates of different education levels. Because of the weight given in the methodology to earnings in the early years of working life, reliance on cross sectional rather than longitudinal data will not unduly distort the 'real' returns. The more well constructed the design of the cross sectional earnings surveys, the more up to date the information and the more realistic it is to assume that in a given country demand and supply in the labour market are major determinants of earnings, the greater can reliance be placed on the results. So far, however, most of the studies which have been made of rates of return in African countries have used seriously deficient data in these respects. As a result the existing studies are insufficient for evaluating investment in higher education and the labour market facing present and future graduates.

Wage Structures

Rates of return attempt to provide a comprehensive view of the economic benefits of educational investments over a lifetime. If reliable calculations of these are generally unavailable for African countries the question arises of whether at least partial and short term assessments of the nature of the labour market facing higher education graduates can be derived from existing data on current earnings structures and recent trends in these.

Surveys of earnings in African countries across both the private and public sectors are virtually non-existent. However, since in only a few countries such as Nigeria and Kenya are higher education graduates employed in the private sector in any significant numbers, it is feasible, in principle, to derive judgements on the labour market for graduates by concentrating on the public sector alone. Even here, however, the available data are very limited and until recently have been largely based on comparisons of starting salaries and points on the salary scales for different education groups.

The most recent survey of public sector earnings across countries comes from an International Labour Office (1982) study covering eight Anglophone countries. Table 4.2 presents graduate starting salaries as a multiple of per capita income in each country. On average, starting salaries were ten times per capita income but the multiples

Table 4.2.   Ratios of Graduate Starting Salary to Per
              Capita Income, 1979

Country	Graduate starting salary: Per capita income
Gambia	11.1
Ghana	3.6
Kenya	14.6
Liberia	11.1
Sierra Leone	5.1
Somalia	8.3
Tanzania	14.2
Zambia	12.0

Source: International Labour Office, (1982).

varied widely from 3.6 in Ghana to over 14 in both
Tanzania and Kenya.   There appears to be no obvious
explanation for such variations in terms of either the
enrolment ratios in higher education or the varying degree
of government wage control.   Beyond concluding that higher
education graduates generally receive earnings far in
excess of per capita income, little can be further gained
from this data.
        More appropriate for the purposes of this study are
data comparing starting salaries of public sector entrants
with different levels of education.   The International
Labour Office study again provides examples.   In Liberia
the starting salary for a university graduate is $6300 as
opposed to a school leaver's $2646.   In Sierra Leone the
corresponding figures are Le.2154 and Le.1446 and in
Tanzania Sh.17,040 and Sh.7800.   These, and other
examples, have been transformed into index number
equivalents and shown earlier in table 2.7.   To recap, in
four of the seven countries surveyed the differentials
received by higher education graduates appear to be
substantial, with earnings for this group around three
times as large as for people who finished their formal
education five or six years earlier.   In the other three
cases – Ghana, Somalia, Zambia – the differentials appear
to be rather narrow.   In Ghana at least this is a result of
substantial falls in the differentials through the 1970s.
Between 1974 and 1980, the university: 'A' level
differential fell by 32 percent and the university: 'O' level
differential by 55 percent.

Earlier work by Jolly (1977) also points to significant falls in the relative position of university graduate earnings. Comparing graduate starting salaries with per capita incomes between approximately 1963 and 1976 for eleven African countries, these fell on average from a multiple of 23 to 16.5. Combining Jolly's data for 1963 with the International Labour Office data for 1979 for Ghana, Kenya, Sierra Leone and Tanzania this differential on average was reduced from 22.4 to 9.4.

The most recent trends in wage differentials by educational level for African countries are provided in studies conducted within the World Bank for Zambia (Meesook and Suebsaeng 1985), Senegal (Bloch 1985), Nigeria (Suebsaeng 1984) and the Sudan (Lindauer and Meesook 1984). Some of the results are shown in table 4.3. The full data for Zambia compare earnings within the government, parastatal and private sectors between 1975 and 1983. Differentials within each sector have narrowed considerably and comparing the earnings of university graduate entrants to the public service with those of the lowest paid salaried employee, the differential has been halved. In Senegal, differentials have also narrowed and, again, most of all for those in the higher occupational levels. The patterns of reduced differentials across all occupational levels, and most noticeably for university graduates, is most vividly demonstrated in Nigeria. In 1965, the graduate entry point salary was six times that of the unskilled worker whereas by 1982 it was only around two and a half times as large. Finally, in the Sudan a similar, if less dramatic, narrowing has again occurred.

Interpretation of all these data causes considerable problems. The apparent general reduction in the premium received by higher education graduates may have been caused by supply increasing at a rate much faster than demand with a consequential tightening of the graduate labour market and the possibility of surpluses existing or being created in the near future. On the other hand, decreased differentials may be solely a result of government wage policy directed at a more equal distribution of income. Despite the problems involved in interpretation, the apparently substantial fall in graduate earnings differentials across a number of countries with differing approaches to the degree of government intervention and control over the economy does suggest that, in large measure, these have resulted from a general and substantial tightening of the labour market for university graduates. The data do not allow a more firm, general conclusion.

As is the case with rate of return studies, analyses

Table 4.3. Indices of Public Sector Salaries by Educational and Occupational Level, Zambia, Senegal, Nigeria and Sudan. Selected Years, 1965-1984

Country & Employment Status	1965	1970	1975	1976	1978	1979	1981	1982	1983	1984
Zambia										
Graduate entry			551					272		
Lowest paid			100					100		
Senegal										
Grade A				493			409			323
Grade B				317			282			238
Grade E				100			100			100
Nigeria										
Graduate entry	600					464		262		
Secondary entry	165					172		117		
Unskilled	100					100		100		
Sudan										
Graduate		386			298				260	
Secondary		215			180				162	
Unskilled		100			100				100	

Source: Zambia; Meesook and Suebsaeng (1985) p.31
          Senegal; Bloch (1985) p.32
          Nigeria; Subsaeng (1984) p.9,10,12
          Sudan; Lindauer and Meesook (1984) p.4,10.

55

of earnings structures can, in principle and under certain conditions, provide a great deal of evidence for judging the behaviour and state of labour markets for higher education graduates. In both cases, however, the existing studies and data for African countries are insufficient for this purpose. Certainly in most countries graduates' earnings differentials have decreased over the past 20 years and, presumably, so have the rates of return on investment in university education. While this suggests that university expansion has often been at a rate not matched by the demand for graduates, neither the amount of data available nor the type are sufficient for detailed judgement. As a result, despite the reservations described earlier regarding estimates of labour shortages and surpluses based on measures such as public service vacancies, levels of expatriate employment and periods of job search this type of information has to be used and is presented in the following section for a number of African countries.

Current Labour Market Balance
        Comprehensive analyses of the current labour market facing higher education graduates using a set of indicators such as vacancies, levels of employment, periods of job search and employment of expatriates exist for very few African countries. The main attempt has been the International Institute for Educational Planning studies of the Sudan, Tanzania and Zambia. The International Labour Office's Jobs and Skills Programme in Africa has surveyed the experiences of graduates from the education system in eight Anglophone countries and in eight Francophone countries but these studies, begun in 1976, focus overwhelmingly on the employment of those with low levels of education. Completed tracer studies of higher education graduates exist hardly at all (an exception being Bardouille 1982 for Zambia). As a result of this lack of analysis, this section relies heavily on individual observers' assessments and on unpublished reports from a variety of sources in an attempt to build up a picture of the current situation. The consequent ad hoc nature of the discussion and the lack of referencing is, therefore, inevitable. The material is first presented by country then aggregated and generalisations drawn.

Botswana. In 1981 there was an estimated shortfall of over 1000 university graduates (demand 1950, supply 900) and projections of needs pointed to an increasing shortfall every year up to 1995. Over this period, expatriate employment was expected to increase. In 1981, expatriates were 61 percent of the Government's professional cadre and 36 percent of Group 'A' officers, while in the private sector, 40 percent of professional and technical positions were similarly filled.

Burundi. Assuming a high rate of economic growth of 5.7 percent a year, a constant level of university entrants and the 1978 entrant:graduate ratio, demand and supply were calculated as follows:

	1978–82	1983–87	1988–92
Demand	900–1100	1000–1200	1100–1600
Supply	1300	1400	1400

This situation would not affect the number of expatriates employed. During the first two years of the 1978–82 Plan, enrolment nearly doubled reaching 3000 in 1979/80. Since then screening is said to have intensified and enrolments have stabilized at around 1200 a year.

Ethiopia. The regulatory mechanisms for skilled manpower allocation result in no analysis of manpower shortages being possible using changes in earnings or unfilled vacancy ratios. An assessment, therefore, was based on requirements and availabilities as recorded by the central allocating authorities. Evidence on the types of skills in short supply was inferred from the extent to which requests for new recruits submitted by ministries, the public service and public corporations were met over the years 1979/80 to 1981/82. The conclusion was that there were real shortages in virtually every field. For the future, however, past increases in enrolments will ease the situation in most areas and it is concluded that unless the economy develops at a much faster rate than in recent years, the projected output should come increasingly closer to meeting the demand for professional personnel. In the meantime, however, the higher education system is said to be far from generating an adequate supply of professional and skilled manpower. The current and future market for higher education graduates, therefore, appears to be good.

Ghana. University enrolments in Ghana in 1985 were below the 1979 level and while there has been little expansion in the economy and labour market over that period, the expected upturn is likely to be met by shortages of graduates.

Guinea. Higher education enrolments between 1968 and 1978 increased by 43 percent a year and as a percentage of the eligible age group are much higher than in most other African countries. Employment in the public sector is guaranteed by law to all those with at least 15 years of education. A recent report argues that the number of university graduates and, to some degree, technicians greatly exceeds the absorptive capacity of the economy which is in virtual stagnation. The 1981–85 plan proposed a reduction of enrolments in higher education institutions by over 40 percent to prevent further overstaffing of the public service.

Lesotho. University enrolments are expected to rise from approximately 900 in 1982/83 to 2030 in 1990 and 4260 in 2000. Services, including Government, constitute the bulk of demand for graduates and 98 percent of all science graduates have been employed in the public service and parastatals. In the future, however, it is expected that non-teaching Government employment for graduates is likely to grow slowly and that most arts and social science graduates will have to take teaching appointments. On the other hand, emigration to South Africa could deplete highly trained labour stocks as demand and wages there are high. With regard to agriculture diploma students, a surplus has already arisen and not all graduates are being employed. As a result of an anticipated further expansion of higher education plus the slowdown in services employment, it is expected that graduates will have to find a new role in industry and agriculture which will call for greater entrepreneurial and organisational abilities in addition to technical skills.

Liberia. There are 5300 expatriate workers of whom 70 percent are in managerial, professional and technical occupations. They hold around 40 percent of all positions at the decisionmaking level and 15 percent of other professional and technical jobs. There is thus a shortage of qualified Liberians, particularly in secondary teaching, the technical professions and all levels of management. At the non-university level, it has been argued that there are sufficient agricultural, vocational and technical education and training programmes to meet what are termed 'basic manpower requirements' in these fields through the 1980s and that improved quality should be the main consideration.

Malawi. Apart from Tanzania, Malawi has the smallest higher education enrolment ratio among 14 East, Central and Southern African countries. In 1979, 13.1 percent (2859) and 42.9 percent (1772) of Professional and Techni-

cal, and Administrative and Managerial workers respectively were expatriate.

Mali. Manpower shortages developed after Independence as
a result of the departure of foreign employees and the
rapid expansion of the economy. Consequently, civil
service employment was offered to all graduates of higher
education. Between 1975 and 1979, the average annual
growth rate for the professional and managerial civil
service category was 23 percent with a high of 30 percent
in 1978/9. In 1983, the government stated that, in the
future, recruitment could only occur when vacancies arise,
reflecting that the excess of higher education graduates
has now become a major social and economic problem.

Nigeria. A situation of unemployment of university
graduates in the late 1960s changed in the early 1970s
when almost all graduates began to gain employment within
90 days of graduation. High level manpower was still said
to be a constraint in 1977 following a government manpower
survey. The survey provided two types of data to justify
this position. The first type was levels of expatriate
employment. In the administrative/managerial category
around a fifth of general managers and managing directors
were non-Nigerian. Among technical professions,
expatriate employment was highest for architects and
electrical engineers. Medicine and university teaching
were also areas of high expatriate employment. The second
set of data was on vacancies. The overall rate in the
modern sector was 23.7 percent, being highest for
secondary school teachers (42.6 percent) and technical,
scientific and professional personnel (41.7 percent).
Despite the shortcomings of these indicators, there were
undoubted shortages of lecturers and of scientific,
technical and medical personnel.
    The Fourth National Development Plan 1981–85
presented the same picture. Despite an enormous increase
in university enrolments from 31,500 in 1975/76 to 57,800 in
1979/80 and in polytechnic enrolments from 8000 in 1973/74
to 35,800 in 1979/80, it was argued that they had not been
adequate to abolish the gap between demand and supply of,
particularly, scientific and technical manpower. This was
especially so in the public sector. For a selected list of
27 high level occupations (omitting teachers and nurses)
the existing stocks were 80,780, existing vacancies were
47,081 and additional requirements 1980–85 to cover
vacancies and new requirements were 96,000. To begin to
meet these estimated requirements, university enrolments
were planned to increase to 109,000 and polytechnic enrol-

ments to 70,000 by 1984/5, while at the same time switching to a higher ratio of science-based courses. Seven new universities of technology were planned. These planned enrolment targets were almost met. However, in 1985 the National Universities Commission reported that only one-third of graduates are now finding employment in jobs that traditionally have been held by them. The situation, it is said, is worst for arts graduates.

Somalia. Since 1981, government employment has been guaranteed to all secondary school and university graduates. However, the recent decline in real wages of government workers has encouraged private sector employment such that hiring levels today remain well below half those in 1978. A recent report provides some manpower forecasts. At the higher education level, the net annual demand for graduates in 1986 is forecast at 154 compared to an outturn of 800. Part of any surplus can be expected to be taken up by employment in Gulf States.

Sudan. The universities have been accused of producing too many graduates in the humanities and too few in the technical areas required by the economy. The situation has been made worse by the emigration to Gulf States of many of the few trained technicians and as a consequence the ratio of technicians to professionals is very low. Enrolments have recently started to shift more towards science and technology but it is argued that the current annual output of agricultural and engineering professionals from the universities and technicians from the higher technical institutes will meet only half of the needs of the Government.

Although the data relate to 1974, the waiting period between graduation and first job for university graduates as described by Sanyal and Yacoub (1975) is interesting. On average, 96 percent of agriculture, engineering and natural science graduates entered employment within six months while 65 percent of graduates of the social sciences and liberal professions did so.

Tanzania. Despite the recent slow growth of the economy, it has been estimated that the gap between supply and demand for high level personnel is higher than anticipated and will persist through the 1980s. Expatriates are widely employed particularly as pharmacists, engineers, technicians, science teachers and in other science based occupations. In addition, vacancies averaging around 30 percent of establishments exist in senior professional jobs and are again highest in those based on science and technology.

Zaire. Automatic guarantees of higher education places to secondary school graduates plus generous living allowances have led to a massive expansion of university enrolments and a recent report points to an oversaturation of the humanities field as opposed to science and administration. High levels of unemployment are reported with most graduates taking an average of one to three years (depending on specialisation) to find employment.

Zambia. The 1977 Manpower Survey indicated that out of a total of 14,936 persons in the high level manpower category, 48 percent were non-Zambian. Major areas of expatriate employment were secondary school teachers and engineers of all types. In proportional terms, the key occupations were metallurgists, architects and physical/life scientists. Annual output of the School of Engineering in 1982 was 30. A sample of 1976 graduates showed that 50 percent entered employment immediately upon graduation, 37 percent within a month and 13 percent between one and six months (Bardouille 1982). Since 1981, however, there have been growing difficulties in placing non-science/engineering graduates, while there are continuing shortages of science/engineering graduates.

Zimbabwe. Until very recently the only certain area of employment for African university graduates was teaching and very few found employment in government or in the private sector (Colclough and Murray, 1979). The situation changed around 1976. In 1979, the output of graduates was 150-200, although another 6000-8000 students were abroad. 16,000 non-Africans were employed in occupations defined as high level. Depending on the degree of naturalisation by non-Africans, the exodus of whites and the numbers of graduates returning from abroad, it is argued that the labour market for higher education graduates should be very open for a number of years.

Table 4.4 summarises the present employment situation for higher education graduates in the countries surveyed above.
In a few countries such as Zaire, Guinea and Mali unemployed higher education graduates are becoming com-

Table 4.4.   Summary of Labour Market Conditions for Higher Education Graduates in 16 African Countries

Country	Comments
Botswana	Very high proportions of expatriates employed and an increasing shortfall of higher education graduates over the 1980s.
Burundi	Forecast demand and planned supply should keep pace implying a constant number of expatriates.
Cameroon	Unemployment of university graduates is emerging.
Ethiopia	Real shortages of higher education graduates in virtually all fields.
Ghana	The present equilibrium in the graduate labour market may be replaced by shortages as the economy expands.
Guinea	Very rapid growth of enrolments has resulted in graduates greatly exceeding absorptive capacity.
Lesotho	The labour market for graduates is tightening. Future vacancies for arts graduates mainly in teaching.
Liberia	High proportions of expatriates employed. Greatest shortages in secondary teaching, technical professions and all levels of management.
Malawi	Large numbers of expatriates employed.
Mali	An excess of higher education graduates is now emerging.
Nigeria	Substantial numbers of expatriates employed and high levels of vacancies identified in the public service particularly for technical,

	scientific and professional person-nel. Massive planned expansion of higher education with slight shift towards science based courses.
Somalia	Manpower requirements for higher education graduates forecast to be well below expected outturn.
Sudan	Substantial over-production of arts based graduates and underproduc-tion of science based graduates. Engineering and agricultural grad-uates meet only half of government needs.
Tanzania	Continued employment of expatriates particularly among engineers, technicians and science teachers. Substantial number of vacancies in science based professions.
Zaire	High levels of unemployment, parti-cularly among humanities grad-uates.
Zambia	Continued shortage of science-based graduates necessitating substantial expatriate employment. Increasing difficulty in absorbing humanities and social science graduates.

monplace. In others, such as Nigeria, Botswana and Ethiopia even high levels of expansion appear copable with for the time being although there are some signs of over expansion in Nigeria. In the largest group of countries, however, the situation appears more mixed and there is concern that the labour market will not be able to absorb the high numbers of humanities graduates in the near future together with an expectation that shortages of science based and professional manpower will remain.

The main determinant of the situation in the labour market facing higher education graduates in the short term is the trend in government employment, largely determined by levels of government expenditure. Governments in five of the 16 countries surveyed have guaranteed employment

employment to graduates and in others the proportions employed in the public service are often very high even without such a guarantee. In Lesotho, for instance, 98 percent of science graduates are employed in the public service and a survey of 900 graduates from the University of Ghana, showed that only 21.5 percent were employed in the private sector (Austin 1985b). Expansion of the public service in most countries was rapid in the 1960s and 1970s as table 2.4 demonstrated but has slowed considerably more recently.

While many parts of the public services are now widely regarded as inflated this is not uniformly the case. Teaching is the prime example. While developed countries have moved towards all-graduate teaching services most African countries are nowhere near approaching this situation. Given the availability of government finance many graduates could continue to find employment in this sector filling new posts and replacing 'under qualified' teachers. Unless graduate wages fall, however, the severe public finance constraint facing most African governments is likely to lead to a blocking off of this area of public employment similar to other areas. The stark reality is that governments can no longer be regarded as willing or able to provide employment irrespective of the skills offered. And no other sector, currently, is filling the governments' place. The result is that apart from the few countries such as Botswana which still employ very large numbers of expatriates and those in which natural resource exploitation has created general expansionary conditions the employment market for graduates, particularly in the humanities and social sciences, can be expected to tighten.

POLICY IMPLICATIONS OF LABOUR MARKET ANALYSIS

The proportion of the relevant age group enrolled in higher education in African countries is very low compared to other regions of the world. Graduate intensity in most parts of most economies is low. Secondary school teaching is commonly dominated by non-graduates. Many countries continue to rely on significant numbers of non-Africans in a wide range of occupations. Planned work schedules in many government departments often imply levels of establishments which are not filled. At the same time, however, governments in many countries cannot afford a general expansion of employment. While the constraint on public expenditure and the relatively small size of the private sector is likely to lead to a tighter labour market all round, the survey of countries suggests that some types of graduates will be affected more than others. This points to an imbalance in the higher education labour market. Before any hasty responses are made to this suggestion, however, the discussion above should be sufficient to indicate one important point. The factual information available in terms of rates of return, wage analyses and systematically collected data on employment indicators is totally inadequate. Monitoring of the outcome of an activity which on average consumes almost 20 percent of the education budget which in turn consumes around 20 percent of total government expenditure is almost non-existent in most countries. In view of the lack of relevant data plus the tentative conclusions which have been reached, recommendations for future actions are made below.

Information Systems
        Better labour market information systems are required for potential students, graduating students and institutions. Conventional manpower requirements fore- casting is insufficient and has the added drawback that any sense of responsibility for the graduating students is taken away from the educational institutions. Ideally, more tracer studies and job evaluations should be undertaken. At the very least, emphasis needs to be placed on documenting labour market experiences during the first year of graduation, or after the period of national service. The possibility of tying receipt of this information to the budgets of institutions could be investigated. Modern sector labour markets are so small in many countries that very fast feedback is required if over- and under-shooting of labour demand is to be avoided. Attention also needs to be given to increasing consultation between educational institutions, the government department responsible for recruitment, major private employers and professional organisations. While employers' employment forecasts can never be regarded as totally accurate, they are potential sources of information which should not be neglected.
        What is essentially being suggested here is the substitution of traditional periodic manpower forecasting exercises by a continuous manpower planning approach. Within this approach emphasis on one planning technique is replaced by an emphasis on planning processes.

Incentives to Students
        As the major employer of most categories of higher education graduates, the government has a large role to play in influencing both the total number of graduates and their specialisation. If, after carefully conducted studies

have been made, potential surpluses and/or shortages of manpower are identified it is possible to alter both the overall incentives to enter higher education and to enter particular faculties. Increasing and varying the costs incurred is one approach. The other is to alter wage structures. In principle, more graduates can be absorbed and utilised in jobs not previously filled by them, the lower the wage. The ability to reduce overall differentials will vary by country and in some countries may be politically impossible. More feasible, however, is a restructuring of starting salaries between occupations providing greater incentives for students to study in areas judged to be suffering from shortages.

Incentives to Institutions

Given what appear to be potential surpluses of certain types of higher education graduates in many countries and the predominance of the public services, any programmes for further expansion of enrolments need to be very closely linked to forecasts of additional government expenditure and the pattern of graduate absorption into the labour market. Apart from providing greater information on current and projected labour market demand to higher education institutions, governments can also attempt to overcome institutional inertia by financial means. Programmes can be provided for retraining staff, special incentives offered for recruiting new staff in priority areas and leverage applied in general to ensure the introduction of new facilities and programmes only in those fields where a proven demand for graduates exists.

Secondary School Science

The employment of expatriates and high levels of reported vacancies in technical positions are widespread across African countries. This does not always imply the need for more places to be created. Many examples exist of unfilled places in high priority subjects in higher education institutions. In particular, faculties of science and engineering often find difficulty in filling places with students having even a minimum qualification in mathematics and general science. In some cases this may be due to a lack of incentive provided by salary structures coupled with a knowledge that failure rates are often extremely high. Mainly, however, it is due to the very small proportions of secondary school graduates who actually possess the basic qualifications. In Nigeria, for example, only 3.5 percent of secondary examination entrants achieve results required for university science courses (Federal Republic of Nigeria 1981a). This results from inadequate science teaching in schools caused by a shortage of qualified science teachers and a severe lack of equipment and materials. Until governments attack this problem with additional incentives and resources, the present lack of graduates with a well rounded science based training will remain.

SUMMARY

Despite its generally low quality, the available information on the current state of the graduate labour market all point to a growing tightening in most fields. This is particularly the case for humanities and social science graduates. For science based graduates the continuing levels of vacancies and expatriate employment reflect the lack of qualified entrants and, perhaps, the quality of higher education teaching more than it does an inadequacy of places. In the immediate future, the expected slow growth of government expenditure and public service employment suggest that a further tightening can be expected. There would, then, appear to be little case for any across-the-board expansion of the higher education sector at the moment.

In the meantime, increased efforts are required to both monitor the immediate experiences of graduates and to develop indicators which will provide signals of imminent changes in the labour market facing them. Added attention needs also to be given to analysing the performance of graduates in employment. These efforts will involve both data gathering and effective consultative procedures. Once a more detailed knowledge of the workings of the labour market has been developed, policies relating to both wage structures and the private costs of education can be developed to influence total demand, and its structure, for higher education. Parallel to these efforts, there is a need to further investigate the internal workings of the higher education sector focussing on increasing the quality of teaching and reducing both student wastage and unit costs. Internal efficiency is the subject of chapter 6. This chapter ends with a brief consideration of the research role of institutions of higher education.

RESEARCH

Universities and polytechnics in African countries have generally been modelled on European and North American lines and are intended to have both a teaching and a research function. As will be shown in chapter 6, student: teaching staff ratios are often very low implying that time

67

is amply available to conduct research. In many institutions, however, the complementary factors of resources and experienced senior staff are not available. As a result, African universities have 'inherited the principle of freedom of research without the means to make it effective' (Yesufu 1973, p.65). The resulting lack of sufficient 'real world' experience by faculty hinders the potential communication to students of how to analyse and solve problems related to the disciplines taught. Courses are often overly theoretical and descriptive rather than oriented to problem solving.

Measuring the quantity and quality of research output of higher education institutions is particularly problematic. Little evaluation of this has been undertaken in the developed countries, let alone in Africa. The potential for organised research, however, has been demonstrated in the past by universities such as Ibadan in Nigeria, Legon in Ghana, Da-es-Salaam in Tanzania and Nairobi in Kenya. Court (1980) briefly describes the current situation in East Africa. A bibliography of research on East African economies showed one out of 50 items contributed in 1963 to have been prepared by African scholars. By 1975, the ratio was 23 out of 92. A similar pattern, he states, occurs in other social sciences and in natural science. A common feature of those universities mentioned above has been the creation of specialised research units, which have gradually built up necessary infrastructure. Court concludes 'Research from being an individual, academic and largely foreign activity has become a sizeable, organised, indigenous and highly valued feature of university life' (1980, p.673). How widely this conclusion applies across African universities is impossible to say.

If research is to remain a major function of higher education institutions then it is necessary that additional resources are provided for equipment, research assistance, data processing and so on. In the more expensive research areas of high technology, cooperative programmes with industry and government appear desirable but in the social sciences, agriculture and the humanities it is possible that small increases in resources could have large payoffs both for purposes of improved teaching and for tackling specific problems. What are required are incentives (or penalties) designed to encourage research plus a framework for allocating additional resources such as through grant-giving research councils. The extent of direct government involvement in directing research to its own priorities is a matter which will have to be determined in an atmosphere of cooperative negotiation between governments and institutions in each country.

There are several ways in which external donors in particular can help facilitate increased and more effective research. These include:

- financing fellowships for study (training and research) abroad and technical assistance for the short-term strengthening of indigenous faculties;
- financing direct research costs (through government research grants);
- financing the provision and strengthening of infra-structure for good teaching, research and knowledge dissemination, such as libraries, documentation cen-tres, and computers;
- encouraging and financing cooperative arrangements for collaboration in research and for the sharing of research results;
- establishing institutional relationships between developed and developing countries on a long-term basis;
- encouraging governments to increase their use of higher education institutions for consulting and research activities and strengthening these institutions where necessary;
- supporting research in priority areas through small non-project-linked grants to scholars in higher education institutions.

Initiatives such as these are based on the pre-condition that research activity continues to be an important inbuilt feature of universities. So far, these institutions have largely been able to defend their research role by arguing that it is necessary if well qualified staff are to be recruited, a truly African body of knowledge developed and students presented with the very latest 'state of the art'. These arguments and the desirability, in principle, of a research role have been widely accepted. What remains at issue is the balance in faculty time devoted to teaching and to research and the degree of orientation of that research towards issues regarded by governments as relevant. In this chapter it has been argued that, for the time being at least, in most countries the economic arguments for a substantial expansion of graduates are weak. A major increase in teaching commitment is therefore unlikely. If this argument is accepted the time is due for a major reconsideration of the ways in which the existing large amounts of faculty non-teaching time can be most efficiently used.

5 Demand and resources for higher education

In the previous chapter, the state of the labour market for higher education graduates in African countries was described. The government is the major employer in almost all of these countries and the rate of expansion of jobs in the public sector has been slowing down considerably in the last few years. However, only in a few, mainly French speaking, countries could it be argued so far that the degree of graduate unemployment is critical. In most others, graduates are not experiencing long periods of unemployment but those with qualifications in the humanities are finding it increasingly difficult to obtain jobs of the type found in the past. This situation, however, is common to many regions – including Western Europe – and does not necessarily imply that this level of education has no economic payoff. What is occurring, however, is that individuals with lower levels of qualifications are being displaced. How this is affecting the private and social rates of return depends for the former on whether graduates receive a salary based on their qualification or on the job they fill, and for the latter on whether there is any increase in the effectiveness with which a job is performed. Neither of these questions can be adequately answered here. Instead, this chapter begins by presenting evidence that enrolments in higher education, and hence the proportion of graduates in the labour force in Africa remain relatively meagre while the social demand for higher education remains substantial. This evidence is then confronted with the macroeconomic and public finance situation facing African governments. This sets the context for the two following chapters which discuss the unit costs of higher education and the possibilities of increasing non-government finance.

SOCIAL DEMAND FOR HIGHER EDUCATION

Higher education enrolments per capita are low in Africa relative to other regions. For every 100,000 population, these enrolments are 139 in Africa, 650 in Asia and the

71

Middle East and 1250 in Latin America. The relatively low levels of higher education enrolments and graduate employment in Africa cannot be explained purely in terms of levels of developent. A comparison of population and primary and higher education enrolments in Nigeria and Pakistan in 1980 illustrates this point (table 5.1). The per

Table 5.1.   Population and Education Enrolments in
Pakistan and Nigeria, 1980

Country	Population (million)	Primary Enrolments (million)	Higher Enrolments (million)
Pakistan	87	6.0	148,000
Nigeria	90	9.5	68,000

Source: UNESCO (1983).

capita income of Pakistan is half that of Nigeria yet, presumably, the government there can finance enrolments and the labour market can absorb increments of higher education graduates well over twice as large.   What are missing from table 5.1 are the unit costs of higher education in the two countries and the salary levels of graduates.   These are returned to later in the chapter.

Reference has already been made to the fact that the educational sector is an interlocking system.   Expansion of one level then increases enrolment demand for the next. Over the period 1970 to 1980 enrolments in secondary education in Africa increased by an average of 13.4 percent a year.   In absolute numbers they increased from 1.4 million in 1965 to 4.8 million in 1975 and to 9.7 million in 1981.   This expansion leads to very strong pressure to increase higher education enrolments.   At present, the proportions of secondary school graduates who continue their studies are relatively low in most African countries. According to UNESCO (1983) data, higher education enrolments as a percentage of secondary enrolments average 5 percent in Western Africa and 7 percent in Eastern Africa compared to 15 percent in Arab countries, 16 percent in Asia and 27 percent in Latin America.   Since the period of study in secondary and higher education and also between countries is dissimilar, these percentages do not provide a clearcut comparison of 'opportunity' but they are indicative of both the small size of the higher education sector in Africa and the pressures to expand.

A more detailed indication of social demand can be seen from data for Kenya, Nigeria and Somalia. In Kenya, secondary school enrolments have escalated rapidly due to the expansion of Harambee 'private' schools. In 1981, at the end of Form Four 11.6 percent of students entered some form of institutional vocational training and 12.3 percent progressed to Forms V and VI. Following Form VI, only 21 percent of those with the minimum required qualifications for university found places, this percentage having fallen from a peak of 30 percent in 1978/9. Another 40 percent or so found places in teacher training institutes, the polytechnics and the institutes of technology (Bertrand and Griffin 1984). It is unlikely that many of the remaining 40 percent did not enter higher education from choice. It should be noted that Kenya has experienced one of the highest rates of economic growth in Africa and therefore has been in a better placed position to expand higher education than most countries.

For Nigeria, two sets of data on 'unsatisfied' demand exist. Ojo (1978) has documented the proportions of qualified applicants who were offered places at three universities in the early 1970s (table 5.2). Since students could apply to several institutions (and since the number of universities now has increased fourfold) the data need care in analysing but they are useful as a rough indication of the situation at that time. More recent data

Table 5.2.   Percentage of Qualified Applicants Receiving University Offers, Nigeria, 1970–74

| Year | University | | | |
	Ife	Ibadan	Lagos	Average
1970	46	32	22	33
1972	17	46	21	28
1974	19	17	36	24

Source: Ojo (1978).

are provided by Adesina (1982) broken down by subject. These are presented in table 5.3.   No description of the

Table 5.3.   Percentage of University Applicants Receiving
Offers by Subject, Nigeria 1979/80

Subject	Offers as Percent of Applications
Agriculture	17.4
Arts	20.6
Business Admin.	8.1
Education	16.6
Law	4.8
Medicine	13.1
Science	40.5
Social Science	12.9
All	15.5

Source: Adesina (1982).

precise nature of these figures or of the way in which they
were derived is provided (though they are discussed
further in chapter 8) but the acceptance rate for science
subjects is double that of any other subject, substantiating
the argument in chapter 4 that the science departments are
being forced to take many poorly qualified students with a
resultant high dropout rate.

Finally, there is similar documentation for Somalia.
In 1983, there were university places for 910 out of 3890
secondary school graduates, or 23.7 percent.   This compares to 33.6 percent in 1981.   If intake levels remain constant, the 'index of opportunity' or percentage of those
qualified who will actually gain places has been calculated
as averaging around 13 percent between 1985 and 1991.

Both the very general ratios of enrolments in higher
to secondary education in sub Saharan African countries
and the three more detailed examples of Kenya, Nigeria and
Somalia point to an excess demand for higher education. An
important set of factors influencing this demand is the
private benefits and costs facing potential students.
Although apparently declining, earnings differentials
remain substantial in many countries.   In chapter 7 it is
shown that private costs, apart from earnings foregone,
are negligible or even negative.

The social demand for higher education has been
shown to be high while, compared to other regions, the
proportions of graduates in the labour forces of sub

Saharan countries are low. The ability of African governments to provide higher education places and employment for the graduates is linked to a single factor – levels of public revenue. The financial situation facing African governments today and in the near future and the likely effects of these on the provision of higher education are discussed below. Prior to that discussion, however, the comparison made earlier between Pakistan and Nigeria is briefly returned to. With a similar population but much lower level of income, the provision of higher education and the absorption of graduates into the labour market was seen to be much greater in Pakistan. This situation can largely be explained in terms of differences in unit costs and the salaries of graduates. In Nigeria, around 1980, unit costs of the universities were US $6000 and in Pakistan, US $360. Graduate entrants to the civil service in Nigeria earned US $6600 a year compared to US $600 in Pakistan. The conclusions are stark – higher education is far more expensive to provide in African countries than in other developing countries and it costs far more to employ the graduates. This leads to a discussion of government finance.

GOVERNMENT FINANCE AND HIGHER EDUCATION

Pressure is being placed on the higher education sector in African countries to produce better trained graduates in more appropriate fields and to increase its level of service to the rest of the community through applied research and greater outreach. There are also significant pressures to expand from secondary school students. These pressures on the higher education sector to expand are being felt at a time when the budgetary constraint in most African countries is tightening.

Economic growth in sub Saharan Africa averaged 5.6 percent a year between 1960 and 1973 falling to an average of 3.7 percent for the rest of the 1970s. In terms of per capita income the seven lowest income countries in the latter period had zero growth, the next 17 countries grew by 1.0 percent, the next 11 by 1.5 percent and the four highest income countries by 3.2 percent. Overall, per capita incomes grew at a mere 1.6 percent a year. More recently, the situation has worsened further with gross national product increasing by only 0.7 percent in 1982, 0.7 percent in 1983 and 1.6 percent in 1984. Per capita incomes have fallen in each year since 1980. The future looks equally bleak, partly as a result of unprecedented falls in the savings rate. In Ethiopia, this fell from 12 percent in 1973 to 3 percent in 1982, in Ghana from 15 percent in 1970 to 3 percent in 1981, in Tanzania from 16 percent in 1967 to 9 percent in 1981, and so on (World Bank 1984a). For the period 1985 to 1995, the World Bank has forecast the average change in per capita income for low-income African countries at between -0.1 and -0.5 percent a year.

While increases in gross national product have been small, pressures to expand government expenditure have remained. For many African countries that has led to an increase in government expenditure as a share of gross national product. The World Bank (1985a) presents these shares for both 1972 and 1982 for nine countries. The averages are 23.8 and 28.1 percent respectively. Of the 18 countries for which data are presented for 1982, eight have government expenditure at levels equal to over 30 percent of gross national product. With slow rates of economic growth and public expenditure shares already high in many countries, pressures to increase public expenditure in the foreseeable future are likely to be resisted.

Turning to education's share of total central government expenditure, the average for sub Saharan African countries in 1980 was 18.9 percent. What is slightly disturbing for the future is that in seven countries for which data on the share are available for 1972 and 1981, it fell on average from 17 percent to 14 percent (World Bank, 1981). At the same time, military expenditure as a proportion of gross national product increased between 1968 and 1978 in 20 out of 33 countries.

Increasing resistance to a further expansion of real education expenditure can be expected to come from two sides. On the one hand, as has been demonstrated, the forecast economic environment for sub Saharan countries is bleak and pressures are to cut rather than expand public expenditure. On the other hand, there is mounting competition from other sectors to take a greater share of any increases and, indeed, to cut into education's existing share. With the school age population increasing each year, the situation in terms of both the expansion of schooling, and the quality, is bleak. With regard to the higher education sector, this is allocated revenue in either of two ways. First, it may compete with other levels of education for a share of a total education budget. Second, it may be considered separately and compete with all other claimants. In both cases, given the nature and range of the criticisms being directed against the sector, its position at present does not appear to be favourable in terms of receiving substantial additional public funds.

In the context of strong social demand for higher

education, comparatively low proportions of graduates in the labour force and a severe financial constraint, there are two possible strategies applicable to the higher education sector in most African countries. The first is to reduce the unit costs but in ways which do not reduce the primary teaching function. The result could then be more graduates for a less than proportional increase in finance or, more ambitious, more graduates for a constant level of finance. The structure of university financing and possibilities of reducing unit costs are discussed in the following chapter (and in the case studies in chapter 8). A second strategy for higher education institutions is to attempt to increase levels of non-government funding, from the private sector, from students and from their own directly economic activities: this strategy is discussed in chapter 7.

6 Unit costs and student wastage

This chapter focusses on the levels and components of unit costs in higher education across African countries, and on student wastage. Policy changes and organisational reforms required to reduce both costs and wastage are then considered. In chapter 8, these issues are taken up again in greater detail concentrating solely on the universities of Ghana and Nigeria.

UNIT COSTS OF HIGHER EDUCATION

Comparisons of annual per student costs in higher education can be illustrated in three ways. First, by a straightforward presentation of the absolute costs converted to United States dollars, second through a comparison with the costs of other levels of education and thirdly through the presentation of the costs as multiples of per capita income. It is the recent emphasis on the latter measure, in particular, which has led to the conception that higher education in Africa is a very high cost activity. All three types of cost measure are produced for 24 African countries and for Asian, Latin American and developed countries in table 6.1. In order to maintain as close a comparability as possible between countries, most of the cost figures used relate to universities alone rather than the more general 'third level'.

Concentrating first on column (1), the absolute unit cost per higher education student in Africa appears to be, on average, similar to that for a student in the developed countries when measured in United States dollars. In some African countries, however, the costs are well above particularly in Zimbabwe, Tanzania and Botswana while in others such as Somalia, Sudan and Ethiopia they are much lower. The similarity of the costs overall between African and developed countries could be viewed as unsurprising given that the institutions perform essentially the same functions, are similarly structured and, in part, recruit staff from a common labour market. However, since the absolute costs of higher education institutions in Asia and

79

Table 6.1. Unit Costs of Higher Education, Selected
Countries and Regions, c.1980

Country/Region	Unit Cost in US $ (1)	Unit Cost as Multiple of Primary Cost (2)	Unit Cost as Multiple of Per Capita GNP (3)
Botswana	6572	42	7.0
Burundi	2928	55	12.7
Ethiopa	1553	57	11.1
Kenya	4149	78	10.6
Lesotho	6167	171	14.2
Malawi	3440	254	15.9
Mauritius	3169	27	2.9
Rwanda	3079	110	14.0
Somalia	895	33	3.2
Sudan	1533	36	4.2
Swaziland	2473	36	3.2
Tanzania	8661	38	30.9
Uganda	2313	385	4.1
Zambia	3750	53	6.5
Zimbabwe	11081	81	12.7
Cameroon	1870	58	2.1
Liberia	4720	102	9.4
Niger	1670	28	5.4
Nigeria	6462	84	7.5
Senegal	1573	13	3.2
Sierra Leone	3332	107	8.5
Togo	2148	56	6.3
Upper Volta	2780	45	13.2
Ivory Coast	5400	39	5.7
Africa	3655	83	8.6
Asia	370		1.18
Latin America	1500		0.88
Developed Countries	3449		0.49

Sources: World Bank (1984a)   Table 1.
            World Bank (1984b)   Table 4.
            World Bank (1984c)   p.33.
            Psacharopoulos (1980) p.23.

Latin America are lower than in Africa such a determinist view should not be taken too far.

An objection to comparisons of the type shown in column (1) is that the widespread existence of overvalued currencies in Africa inflates the unit cost estimates. Concern, however, does not decrease if comparisons across countries and regions are made, not in absolute terms, but in terms of 'affordability' and opportunity cost. The data in columns (2) and (3) give indications of these. Column (2) which compares unit costs in primary and higher education in some cases underestimates total primary school costs since the multiples are based on government costs alone and in a number of countries local communities and/or religious bodies also finance primary schools. On average, however, government costs of one place in higher education are equivalent to 83 places in primary school (the median is 55). Column (3) focusses on higher education costs in relation to total resource availability as measured by per capita gross national product. In these terms, on average a higher education place in Africa consumes a share of total resources 17 times greater than in developed countries, almost ten times greater than in Latin American countries and seven times greater than in Asian countries.

The absolute cost figures in column (1) are averages across subjects. Although, on the whole, the distribution of students by subject in African countries does not vary greatly from other regions (Psacharopoulos 1980) and is not therefore a cause in itself of the relatively high average costs, variations in departmental costs across subjects are interesting to examine. These are shown for six African countries in table 6.2. While reservations must exist over the raw data used, it is clear that the actual distribution of students across faculties will have a very large effect on average unit costs since science based subjects appear to be two to three times as expensive as arts based ones.

Determinants of Unit Costs

Previous chapters have illustrated that the development of the higher education sector in Africa has been very recent. Nigeria's experience of one university in 1959 and over 20 today highlights this point most dramatically. Not only are most institutions new, many have small numbers of enrolments - between one and two thousand in a majority of countries. It may be, therefore, that the current high unit costs can be partly explained by the non-realisation of economies of scale. Such an explanation usually goes together with an expectation that

81

Table 6.2. Higher Education Unit Costs by Subject (Humanities = 100)

Country	Humanities	Social Science	Law	Education	Science	Agriculture	Engineering	Medicine
Lesotho	100	66	72	148	133	–	–	–
Sudan	100	83	85	100	86	95	88	136
Somalia	100	58	87	89	–	184	–	198
Tanzania	100	100	93	–	647	912	120	–
Kenya	100	100	–	–	191	260	–	208
Zambia	100	100	76	–	–	212	115	292
Average	100	84	83	116	264	333	108	208

Source: World Bank estimates for Lesotho, Sudan, Somalia and Tanzania.
Psacharopoulos (1980) table 5.2. for Kenya and Zambia.

these economies will occur in the future as expansion proceeds. Whether this is likely to be so can be partially tested in two ways: first by comparing enrolment and unit cost relationships across countries and second by examining the movement of unit costs over the recent past within individual institutions.

To test whether there is any relationship across countries between the levels of enrolments and unit costs a simple linear regression analysis was made for 18 African countries with actual unit costs (UC), the dependent variable and enrolments (E), the independent variable. The results are shown below:

$$UC = 3259 + 0.032E \qquad R^2 = 0.06$$
$$(5.903) \quad (1.012)$$

Numbers in parenthesis are t-ratios. There appears to be no statistical relationship between the actual cost and enrolments. This corroborates Psacharopoulos' (1980) calculation for developing countries as a whole, although in his case the addition of enrolment squared and per capita income variables did produce statistically significant results with an R^2 of 0.21. Similarly, calculations using average cost as a multiple of per capita income also led to statistically significant results indicating decreasing 'costs' for higher levels of enrolment.

Whatever the results of such cross country regressions, there is no inevitability that unit costs of individual institutions will or will not decrease as enrolments expand. Institutions tend to have a dynamic of their own. Recent experiences within higher education institutions may, therefore, prove a better guide to what may be expected to happen to costs in the future in the absence of specific policy changes. Some examples are provided below:
- in Lesotho, unit costs at constant prices increased by 75 percent between 1969 and 1982 while enrolments rose from 386 to 1133;
- in Kenya, the University of Nairobi witnessed a decline in unit costs over the 1970s leading to reductions in teaching materials and only 20 percent of the proposed research programme being funded;
- in Tanzania, the current budget for the University of Da-es-Salaam increased by 418 percent and enrolments by 134 percent between 1971 and 1979;
- in the Sudan between 1973 and 1976, the higher education budget grew faster than the combined growth of enrolments and the cost of living.

These experiences are not sufficient to indicate any definite trends in the effects increased enrolments have had

83

on unit costs. Another, very approximate, measure of
trends in costs is derived from changes in student:teaching
staff ratios. Again, data are scarce but the figures
provided by Court (1980) for Nairobi, Da-es-Salaam and
Makerere for the period 1965 to 1979 are not encouraging
(table 6.3).

Table 6.3.   Student:Teaching Staff Ratios at the
Universities of Nairobi, Da-es-Salaam and Makerere,
1964-79

| University | Student:Staff Ratios | | |
	1965	1971	1979
Nairobi	6.3	6.9	5.6
Da-es-Salaam	7.3	6.8	6.2
Makerere	9.0	7.4	5.9

Source: Court (1980) p.669.

On the basis of the data available for individual
African countries it is not possible to definitively judge
whether in the past, economies of scale have operated
within higher education. On balance the evidence suggests
that they have not.   That there are possibilities of
reducing unit costs without a serious deterioration in
educational quality, however, is very clear from examining
current practices within a sample of African universities.
These are discussed below under the headings of student:
teaching staff ratios, salaries and expatriate employment,
non-academic expenditures and utilisation rates.

Student:Teaching Staff Ratios. For 51 universities in 30
countries, the median student:teaching staff ratio in the
late 1970s was 8:1 according to the Association of African
Universities (1983). (See Appendix Table A3.) In table
6.4, both average and subject specific ratios are presented
for twelve countries using a different set of sources and,
in most cases, more up to date information.   The average
student:teaching staff ratio for the twelve African countries
sampled is again 8:1. This is well below the ratios in
other parts of the world including the developed countries.
The problems obviously lie most acutely in the science
departments where the average ratio is 5:1 - half that in
the United Kingdom - but there are also examples of
extremely low ratios in a wide range of other subjects.

Table 6.4.   Student:Teaching Staff Ratios by Country and Subject

Country	Year	Average	Subject		Subject	
Lesotho	1982	8.6	Science	7.4	Education	4.6
			Soc.Science	11.9	Law	12.9
			Humanities	7.7		
Botswana	1982	8.8	Humanities	6.5	Science	4.7
			Soc.Science	10.0		
Malawi	1981	8.3	Fine Art	1.0	Physics	3.9
			Philosphy	2.5	Chemistry	4.7
			English	10.0	Economics	10.0
			Engineering	6.2	Agriculture	9.5
Tanzania	1982	4.0	Agriculture	2.0	Engineering	6.0
			Arts	3.0	Medicine	2.0
			Soc.Science	3.0	Commerce	15.0
Kenya	1982	9.5	Agriculture	5.2		
		12.5	Medicine	3.4		
Sudan	1976	9.6				
Mauritius	1979	5.4				
Rwanda	1980	7.0				
Burundi	1982	7.1				
Uganda	1978	5.9				
Somalia	1983	5.7	Languages	5.3	Medicine	4.1
			Engineering	7.9	Agriculture	3.9
Ghana	1984	13.2				
Average Africa		8.1				
United Kingdom		12.0				
United States		15.0				
France		15.0				

Note: Where more than one figure exists for a country, each relates to an individual institution.

Sources: World Bank (1977) Table 5 and 12 Sudan.
           World Bank (1984b) Table 19. Mauritius,
                   Burundi, p.42 France, United States.
           World Bank (1984c) Table T.23 Malawi.
           World Bank (1984d) p.12 Lesotho.
           Court (1980) p.669 Uganda.
           World Bank, UNESCO and USAID estimates
                   Botswana, Kenya, Tanzania, Rwanda,
                   Somalia.

Even in a university as long establised as Da-es-Salaam, student:staff ratios in the humanities and social science faculties were only 3:1 in 1980. The potential for either reducing staff or increasing enrolments at well below current average teaching costs obviously exists.

Salaries and Expatriate Employment.   Student:teaching staff ratios are an important determinant of unit costs because of the high teaching salaries and extensive fringe benefits relative to per capita incomes.   African universities did not expand gradually as in a number of Asian and Latin American countries and their establishment required large numbers of expatriate lecturers. Recruitment, therefore, was on the international market and salaries and conditions were set accordingly. In addition, for whatever reasons, public sector salaries as a whole were set at levels above per capita incomes to a degree much greater than in other developing regions.   While we do not have comparative data on current university teacher salaries, Eicher (1984) has demonstrated the relatively high salaries of primary school teachers in Africa.   These average 6.7 times per capita income, compared to 2.4 times in both Asia and Latin America.   Similarly, Tait and Heller (1983) show that in Francophone and Anglophone Africa, civil servants' salaries average 9.6 times and 4.6 times per capita income respectively, while in Asia the multiple is 2.9 and in Latin America 3.1.   While there is no reason to believe that university salaries in African countries are above those earned at a similar level in the rest of the economy, their size is one cause of the high unit cost.

    The continued widespread employment of expatriates is another cause of high costs mainly because of the additional non-salary costs.   Compared to the rest of the public sector and the private sector, the proportions of expatriates in university teaching are commonly high.

86

Again, Court (1980) provides relevant data for three East African universities between 1965 and 1979 (table 6.5). While the proportions of non-East Africans employed fell over this period they still provided a majority of faculty in 1979. More recent data for Da-es-Salaam show that

Table 6.5. Non-East Africans as a Percentage of Academic Establishments, Nairobi, Da-es-Salaam, Makerere, 1965-79

	1965	1971	1979
Nairobi	81	69	61
Da-es-Salaam	84	68	46
Makerere	83	73	84

Source: Court (1980) p.669.

expatriates now form 37 percent of the teaching staff and if medicine is omitted, 23 percent. Expatriate intensity also varies by subject in Kenya. The range is from 69 percent in science to 50 percent in arts and social sciences.

Universities in other countries have similarly high levels of expatriate employment. In 1979, non-Africans filled an average of 33 percent of posts in 30 universities in 18 countries (Appendix Table A3). Current examples are Somalia 26 percent, Nigeria 28 percent, Ethiopia 40 percent and Rwanda 48 percent. On the whole it appears that expatriates still hold between a quarter and a half of all teaching positions in most African countries. As these proportions fall, so should unit costs.

Non-academic Expenditures. While student:teaching staff ratios may be low and salaries relatively high, direct departmental teaching costs are often a surprisingly low proportion of total costs. At the University of Lesotho, the proportion is 34 percent and at the University of Khartoum, 42 percent. Teaching and research costs at the University of Malawi are again around 40 percent of total costs, most of the rest being spent on travel allowances, transport, administration, maintenance and student living and allowances. The case studies of Ghanaian and Nigerian universities also corroborate this pattern. One reason for high non-teaching costs is the employment of large numbers of non-teaching staff. At the University of Khartoum in 1976 the total number of employees was 5892 to support 7600 students. A similar situation exists at the University of

Da-es-Salaam where there are two non-teaching staff to each faculty member. The result is to produce an overall student:staff ratio of only 1.4:1. In Nigeria's universities in 1980–81 there were 77,000 students and 52,000 staff.

Large numbers of non-teaching staff are not the only cause of high non-teaching costs. Many African universities have taken on functions which are absent in universities in other parts of the world with the result that many campus' are virtually townships. Staff housing is one example. In Kenya, for instance, the University of Nairobi owns 200 houses and rents another 730. Staff housing is commonly heavily subsidised. Other facilities often provided free or at low cost by universities include schools, medical centres and staff clubs. All of these add significantly to unit cost per student.

Another widely observed major cause of the high unit costs of higher education to governments in African countries is the often free provision of student living facilities coupled with student allowances. This issue will be examined in greater detail in chapter 7 but is introduced here. Acharya (1982) has shown that a sample of Francophone governments in the late 1970s spent an average of 43 percent of the higher education budget on scholarships and social expenditures and Anglophone governments, 14 percent. These compared with 4 percent for a sample of Asian countries. In 1978 in Mali, scholarships in higher education were equal to 45 percent of the total education budget, although by 1982 the percentage had fallen to 29.0. Students at the University of Ougadougou in the Upper Volta (now, Burkina Faso) in 1981 received stipends equal to 770 percent of GNP per capita. As a whole, these were equal to 81 percent of the total primary school budget. In Zaire, allowances are higher than the average primary school teacher's salary.

Utilisation Rates. The low student:faculty ratios described above are partly a result of the attempted provision of a very wide variety of courses. At the University of Lesotho, for example, 142 courses are offered in students' final year with an average enrolment of 15. In some cases, even though student:staff ratios are low, student contact hours are also low. At the University of Malawi these range between eight and twelve hours a week (World Bank 1984c). This situation points to an under-utilisation of faculty. Other measures of utilisation concern the institutions' physical facilities. The evidence is mixed. A case study has been prepared for the University of Lesotho where unit costs have been increasing as enrolments have grown (World Bank 1984d). During term time, the average classroom use is 74 percent and laboratories are used for 57 percent of the time. However, because of small classes only 44 percent of places are on average occupied. Given these use factors and calculating over a whole year, only 31 percent of capacity is taken up. Obviously there are severe constraints to substantially increasing classroom use in term time but once again the potential exists for changes which would result in a decrease in unit costs. At other higher education institutions, however, there are reports of overuse of existing facilities. Pressures on facilities such as libraries are reported for Kenya where enrolments (at Kenyatta University) are already 20 percent higher than planned. Student contact hours there are significantly greater than those reported for Malawi – social science 24 hours, agriculture 27 hours, engineering 31 hours, science 26 hours. Similarly, the University of Dakar in Senegal was originally planned for 3500 and now holds 8000 students.

A Warning
     So far in this chapter it has been shown that from almost any standpoint unit costs of higher education are high in African countries and the reasons for these have been described. There are also, however, widespread reports of overcrowding, curtailment of research funding, cutbacks in staff development programmes and few books, periodicals and teaching materials. Recent descriptions of the situations in universities provide examples. An article in West Africa (18 July 1983) describes the students at the University of Kumasi in the following way "...they are attending a university which is grossly short of staff, books, paper and food". A recent unpublished report describes Addis Ababa University in Ethiopia in a similar way,

     There is overcrowding in many of the faculties. Further-
     more, many students are unable to obtain essential
     textbooks in their subject. Overcrowding and overuse of
     equipment as well as a lack of relevant study materials
     are bound to have an impact on the quality of
     educational output.

Similarly, the Vice Chancellor of Fourah Bay in Sierra Leone is reported as describing a situation in which university budget estimates 'pared to the bone' of 11.5 million leones were cut to 9.5 million, then 7.5 million (West Africa, 23 January, 1982).
     These descriptions, and those provided for Ghanaian and Nigerian universities in a later chapter, are important

89

antidotes to the impression that since unit costs are high, all forms of reduced funding will have no effect on the quality of education. African universities have evolved in the context of a set of ideas which have given them welfare responsibilities in addition to educational responsibilities and it is extremely important that in any discussions of the causes of high costs, these are separated.

STUDENT WASTAGE

Internal efficiency measures for higher education are not confined to analysing resources per student. It is also important to assess the extent to which students graduate from their courses, and the degree of repetition of course years. For the higher education sector in Africa two different types of comparison can be made to set the context. In the United Kingdom, 94 percent of all first year students graduate after three years. On the other hand dropout and repeater rates at primary and secondary schools in Africa are very high. In 15 Eastern African countries, the average completion rate for the primary cycle is 65 percent and for ten Western African countries it is 47 percent.

Turning to examples of higher education student wastage in individual countries, dropout rates in Kenya are reported to have been relatively high up to 1975 but to have fallen since (World Bank 1980). They were highest in architecture (20 percent), engineering (14 percent) and agriculture (10 percent), but are currently at around 6-8 percent in these subjects. Repetition rates have also fallen. In 1970, 18 percent of final year engineering students were repeaters while in 1980 the figure was down to 10 percent. In the social sciences and sciences, repeaters now make up between 1 and 3 percent and 1 and 4 percent of total enrolments a year respectively.

The situation appears to be considerably worse in a number of other countries as table 6.6 indicates. In Zambia, dropout and failure rates are reported to be: sciences 48 percent, engineering 40 percent, education 28-39 percent, law 25 percent, humanities 19 percent and agriculture 17 percent (Psacharopoulos 1980). Graduation rates at the University of Khartoum average 65 percent ranging from 46 percent in geology to 81 percent in law. For several countries, wastage is particularly high at the end of the first year. In Burundi, the rate is almost 50 percent, at Addis Ababa 35 percent, in Zaire 62 percent and in Zimbabwe 71 percent. Although wastage rates in only seven countries have been presented, the picture is very bleak. Of these countries, only in Kenya are rates

Table 6.6.   University Wastage Rates by Year and Subject,
                   Selected Countries

| Country | Subject | | | | First Year | Overall |
	Engineering	Law	Humanities	Agriculture		
Zambia	40	25	19	17		30
Sudan	48	19		44		45
Burundi					50	
Ethiopia					35	49
Zaire					62	68
Zimbabwe					29	

Source: World Bank and UNESCO estimates.

apparently under control and in the rest they appear to be between one third and two thirds. The high unit costs per student then translate into enormous unit costs per graduate.

There are four possible causes of high wastage rates — financial pressure, inadequate prior preparation in secondary schools, low teaching quality in higher education and inappropriate standards for promotion and graduation. The low level of direct costs to students in higher education and the large returns upon graduation suggest that in all but the most extreme case, financial hardship is not a major cause of dropout. The main causes lie within the education system. Secondary schools in many African countries are often inadequately staffed with unqualified teachers and suffer from a lack of teaching materials. Combined with poor primary schooling and non-supportive home backgrounds, the educational outcomes are often inadequate as a base for higher education. This is especially the case for science subjects. However, because of the policy of many governments of enrolling increasing proportions of students in science faculties, entrance requirements are often low. Once in higher education, the educational deficiency may not be corrected. Despite the excellent staff development programmes of some institutions, the rapid expansion of universities may in some cases have led to the appointment of poorly qualified and inexperienced faculty. In addition, teaching methods may be ineffective and performance evaluation not conducted in time for remediation. Finally, institutions may be continuing to use promotion and graduation standards adopted from European countries which are unnecessarily restrictive. Some of these causes of high wastage rates will take many years to cure. Others, however, can to some extent be remedied.

POLICIES TO INCREASE INTERNAL EFFICIENCY

Unit costs of higher education in African countries are typically high and there is pressure to reduce them. The already high wastage rates, however, and reports of poor teaching conditions imply that in reducing costs great care needs to be taken to ensure that the quality of teaching does not fall. While this does not necessarily mean that the level and composition of direct teaching resources need to be left totally unchanged it does imply that greater emphasis should be given to reducing the non-teaching expenditures borne by the universities.

Faculty:student ratios are extremely high in many departments in many universities. Partly these result from a high degree of specialisation relative to the number of students in each major area. Minimum sizes for classes and departments need to be set and targeted faculty: student ratios consciously moved towards by non-renewal of contracts, a reconsideration of tenure arrangements, encouragement of secondment and the re-direction of faculty to sponsored research, together with a careful expansion of enrolments in high priority subjects. This may involve combining small departments and requiring faculty to teach in other than specialist areas. In the larger countries, institutions could be encouraged to specialise more on a narrower range of subjects while small countries could share facilities. In the past, regional universities such as the University of East Africa comprising campus' in Nairobi, Da-es-Salaam and Makerere, and the University of Botswana Lesotho and Swaziland have not been able to sustain themselves. Today's financial constraints, however, may provide a new stimulus. Another alternative is to continue sending students abroad for study. Both these options require detailed research.

The possibilities of reducing repetition rates by altering university regulations have been demonstrated in Kenya. Existing regulations governing promotion and graduation need to be reviewed in many countries to assess whether they could be eased without too great an effect on the eventual capabilities of graduates. Conversely, 50 percent dropout rates at the end of first year courses indicate that in some countries admission criteria need to be re-examined. The requirement to expand higher education science courses while secondary school science achievement remains low points to a need to re-appraise the nature and objectives of first year programmes.

The utilisation rates of physical facilities vary widely. In some institutions classrooms and libraries are grossly overcrowded while in others space, particularly in laboratories, is under-used. In some cases, higher enrolments could be easily accommodated in existing facilities while in others, lack of facilities is a major constraint to expansion. In all cases, better scheduling and a concentrated effort by individual faculties and departments to share facilities could improve efficiency. More radical would be the use of new teaching technologies such as those initiated by the United Kingdom's Open University or the Ramkhambaeng University in Thailand whose enrolments now reach 115,000. Even those universities where term time utilisation rates are high, and even excessive, generally operate at these levels for only parts of the year. Thirty-week teaching years make little sense in countries with such low levels of resources. Faculty should not provide a constraint to lengthening the teaching year. While African universities had to compete in a tight international academic labour market in the 1960s and offer conditions similar to those in developed countries, this market has substantially tightened. Even in cases where longer teaching years for faculty could not be implemented, there is room for experimenting with four-term university years with each faculty member taking only three or with a double annual intake of students and more regular periods of study leave.

Most of the policies suggested above to reduce unit costs involve an expansion of enrolments and would not lead to decreases in the overall level of government resources used in higher education. To do that would require the whole issue of university and government expenditure in areas not directly related to teaching and research to be opened up to discussion. Student finance will be considered at length in the following section. There are other areas, however. Subsidised staff housing is an example. Automatic study leave with travel entitlements is another. Full salary while undergoing further study abroad is yet another, and the provision of university funded schools for faculty children again requires a fresh look. The apparently inflated numbers of non-teaching staff documented earlier for several universities suggest that substantial savings could also be made in this area. In addition, there is scope for many service units to become self financing and for departments to generate their own income. All these possibilities are discussed in detail in chapter 8.

A second way in which inefficiencies can be reduced is through measures designed to strengthen the management of the total system of higher education. The multi-objectives which higher education institutions aim, and are expected, to fulfil and the autonomy which many have preserved lead to managerial complexity. In the context of external demands to take on an increased developmental and outreach role in addition to the requirement to give high quality teaching, institutions need to more clearly define their objectives and roles. The wide range of services which many remain responsible for beyond the provision of education and research facilities makes day to day management even more demanding than in many developed countries and places a strain on senior administrators who are often not supported by sufficiently experienced staff. Again adopting practices of institutions in developed countries, administrations are often staffed on the basis of academic credentials rather than managerial skills and proven experience. While many universities have undertaken substantial programmes of staff development for faculty, often with foreign donor support, few have developed such programmes for administrative staff.

The potential which exists for cost reductions and increased student flows requires that reliable information systems exist and that effective cost control and budgeting systems are in operation. Case studies of the management of universities (Kenya, Tanzania, Malawi, Lesotho) all point to a lack of these. For the University of Nairobi it is argued that the accounting and information support systems for planning and budgeting are absent and that a priority should be the tracking of efficiency indicators to aid admission policies, the determination of faculty budgets, staff requirements and so on (World Bank 1980). In a recent (1982) report prepared by the University of Da-es-Salaam for President Nyerere, serious weaknesses in financial control are admitted. Similarly, at the National University of Lesotho, it is argued that the planning and budgeting process is not carried out systematically and that measures of staff:student ratios, graduate output, research, and so on, are not being used to justify departmental budgets (World Bank 1984d). Some of these universities are among the more established ones in Africa and it is unlikely that the situation is very different elsewhere.

The decisionmaking autonomy which universities, in particular, enjoy is based on the principle that they are able to manage their activities efficiently without significant government involvement. At a time of increased financial constraint, more attention is likely to be focussed by governments on this principle. It is in the interests of higher education institutions, therefore, to begin to implement systematic evaluations of teaching programmes covering aspects such as objectives, staffing, enrolments, wastage, placement, manpower needs, relationships to other programmes and institutions and student and faculty achievement.

To conclude this chapter, it is useful to present the results of two exercises which have attempted to calculate the financial and enrolment effects of introducing the types of cost cutting measures described earlier.

At the University of Lesotho in 1982, overhead costs totalled 4.2 million maloti. According to a World Bank study, an estimated saving of 1.1 million maloti could be made through: the elimination of leased housing, full costing of the primary school and printshop, privatisation of the refectory, garage and maintenance and stores units, the reduction in student residence staff and a small increase in lodging fees (World Bank 1984d). In addition, it is calculated that teaching staff:student ratios of 1:10 in science and 1:12 elsewhere could support a student population of 1574 as against the present 1154 resulting in a reduction of 10 percent in overall unit costs. Taking the 1980/1 budget of the University of Malawi, a similar World Bank study estimated that a 20 percent reduction in total costs would have resulted from a decrease in the staff: student ratio to 1:10 in most departments and 1:12 in a selected few, reduced salaries for faculty training abroad, reduced travel and transport costs and the restriction of allowances to 25 percent of students (World Bank 1984c). An alternative way of viewing the effects of decreased teaching staff:student ratios is to argue that at 1:10 and 1:12 ratios, 2260 and 2712 students could have been accommodated respectively compared to the actual 1912 in 1982.

These rough calculations imply that significant public expenditure savings of around 20 percent could be made by changes which would still result in teaching staff:student ratios being higher than in many European universities, continued substantial subsidisation of students and non-wage staff benefits beyond those of most of the rest of the working population. It is evident that the scope for cost reduction exists.

7 Alternative sources of finance

The fundamental set of factors in higher education facing most African governments is that while there are often both social and economic pressures to expand enrolments, budgetary revenues available for the sector are not increasing at the same rate. One response is to attempt to reduce the unit costs. Another, not an alternative, is to investigate whether part of the cost of higher education can be funded through non-government sources of revenue. These could include the operation of private universities in which student fees cover the costs, contributions to the funding of particular aspects of public universities from industry and commerce, additional funds raised by the universities' own activities and the charging of tuition fees and/or fees for food and accommodation to students in public universities.

PRIVATE INSTITUTIONS

Privately owned and managed institutions of higher education are common in a number of South East Asian and Latin American countries. In Africa, such institutions exist hardly at all. There are two main reasons for this lack. The first is the ethos inherited from European colonial governments after the second world war that social services are the responsibility of the state. As the gradual take over from the churches of many primary and secondary schools indicates, this view has if anything grown stronger since independence. One of the few instances in Africa of a government encouraging the growth of private universities was in Nigeria in the late 1970s. This policy has now been reversed on the grounds of the difficulty of controlling educational quality. The second reason for the virtual non-existence of private higher education institutions is financial. As was shown in chapter 6, this level of education is expensive to provide in Africa. Private institutions would need to charge substantial fees to cover the costs. While the public sector institutions continue to provide free education there is

97

little chance that fee charging ones could emerge. In the context of African incomes, these could only develop alongside arrangements which provided students with access to loans.

PRIVATE SECTOR CONTRIBUTIONS

In principle, the private sector could contribute to the costs of higher education in a number of ways beyond its existing contribution via taxation. The contributions could be piecemeal or generalised. In the first category, large firms could be encouraged or required to help fund those faculties from which they recruit graduates, particularly when such faculties are very specific such as mining engineering or rubber technology. Instances of this practice are very few. Alternatively, firms might be encouraged to offer high level training themselves as do the multinational mining companies in Liberia. More generalised schemes could include the provision of bursaries or scholarships to at least partially replace government subsidies or, alternatively, finance might be generated through some form of graduate-hiring tax. The feasibility and employment effects of this would depend on the tightness of the labour market and the ability of employers to alter earnings structures. One of the areas which is likely to become (even more) underfunded in a period of constraint or cutting of university finance is research. A recent commission investigating academic salaries and conditions of employment in Nigeria has suggested the imposition of an earmarked levy on the private sector for university research (Federal Republic of Nigeria 1981b). For the present, the Government has rejected the proposal.

Schemes along these lines are unlikely to provide substantial resources since in only a few African countries is the private sector a major employer of higher education graduates. While efforts should be made to analyse the feasibility and consequences of increasing the private sector's contribution, the results are not likely to be significant.

INCREASED INSTITUTIONAL FUNDS

Comparing the sources of funding in British and Nigerian universities Oduleye (1985) has shown that the government contribution is 76 and 91 percent respectively. Most of the difference results from external funding of research. While the opportunities to tap funding for research in African universities may not be so straightforward, there are

591 92189

opportunities for them to utilise their often comparatively
vast amount of talent and, in some cases, resources.
Twenty-eight or 30 week teaching years also provide the
time for faculty and non-teaching staff in both teaching
departments and service units to engage in work having a
monetary payoff. Universities in both Ghana and Nigeria
have become involved in such activities and their
experiences are documented in the case studies in chapter
8. Activities in just one university include the
manufacture and sale of beds, chairs, soap, pumps and
traffic lights, the rearing of cattle, fish and poultry, a
300 acre oil palm project and servicing of fridges,
freezers, air conditioners and motors. While there needs to
be an awareness of the possible detrimental educational
consequences of these activities, it is becoming obvious, at
least in Ghana and Nigeria, that the resources of the
universities themselves can be used to generate additional
funds.

STUDENT CONTRIBUTIONS

With the advent of the current world recession, the severe
restraint on government finance felt throughout the Third
World and the current vogue among Western governments
and international development agencies to lay greater
stress on the play of markets, there has been a recent
upsurge in interest in the possibility of implementing
schemes of 'cost recovery' and 'user cost charges' in the
social services. Not surprisingly, one of the areas which
has attracted attention in this way is higher education. In
general, proposals have come in two forms. First, the
straightforward charging of fees for tuition and for
accommodation and food. This proposal is often coupled
with a scholarship scheme for the poorest students. The
second proposal is for a system of student loans which
again would cover living expenses and perhaps some
proportion of direct teaching costs and would be available
for all students. Before turning to the arguments for and
against such user cost schemes and their feasibility, the
current financial arrangements for students in higher
education in 24 African countries are summarised below.

Botswana. The university charges fees for tuition and for
room and board. Bursaries to cover these plus the
purchase of books and supplies and an allowance for
personal expenses are available to all who apply. In
return, graduates are bonded to the government for a
period equal to the length of their course plus one year

and pay back 5 percent of their salary annually during that period. Students abroad have the same conditions attached to their bursaries.

Burkina Faso (Upper Volta). In addition to free tuition, students at the University of Ougadougou receive allowances equal to 770 percent of per capita income. Scholarships at secondary and higher education constitute 35 percent of total educational expenditure.

Burundi. Free tuition. Between 1977 and 1979, the total value of Government fellowships for living expenses quadrupled.

Cameroon. Only half of all students receive scholarships and a lack of finance is suggested as a major reason for high rates of student wastage. In the professional institutes, all students receive a scholarship.

Ethiopia. Although part time students who attend evening classes pay fees, full time students do not.

Ghana. This country is one of the few to have introduced a comprehensive loan scheme for students. It was begun in June 1971 and abandoned in October 1972. The loans were to cover board and lodging plus other personal expenses. The National Consultative Committee on Educational Finance in 1975 recommended the reintroduction of loans but this did not occur. More recently (March 1984) the National Education Commission again recommended a loan scheme for maintenance and personal expenditure. At present, tuition, lodging and two meals a day are free and each student receives a book allowance of 900 cedis (US $10). A two year period of national service is required from each graduate.

Ivory Coast. In 1985, the Government dropped its policies of allowing all students who successfully completed secondary school to enter university and allocating scholarships to every student. Of 3200 students accepted into Abidjan University, 2500 received scholarships allocated according to their academic record, families' financial situation and subject of study.

Kenya. Loans have been frequently suggested for Kenyan students (Rogers 1972, Fields 1974) but only a very limited scheme to cover living expenses exists. Since this was established in 1974 K sh.21 million (US $1.5 million) have been loaned. However, in 1981 while 540,025 sh. were due for repayment, only 99,408 sh. were collected. Woodhall (1983) reports that an attempt in 1981 by the Government to introduce a clause making parental land a collateral provoked demonstrations and was dropped. Almost as many Kenyans study at overseas universities as study in Kenya and it is instructive to note that 90 percent of these students are paying tuition costs and bearing living expenses.

Lesotho. Around 86 percent of students receive loans of M1,081 (US $1,178) a year, one third of which is paid directly to the university to cover partial costs of tuition and dormitories. The present scheme is for the loan to be repaid in equal annual instalments over five years with a 50 percent remission if graduates work for the government. The enforcement procedures are, again, inefficient. Although the scheme has been in operation since 1977 and total loans in 1983-4 were M1.4 million only around M10,000 a year is currently being collected.

Malawi. Tuition, board and lodging are free and in addition, all students are awarded allowances of K215 a year (US $172). The allowances equal 6.2 percent of the university's budget. Boarding costs per student are K312, and form 8.5 percent of the university's total recurrent costs. The Government has recently announced its intention to charge fees for board and lodging.

Mali. Reference has previously been made to secondary and higher education scholarships being equal to almost 43 percent of the education budget. In the past, any actions to change the scholarships policies have met with serious opposition in the form of student strikes and riots. However, changes to the eligibility criteria for foreign scholarships have mainly been responsible for the fall in scholarships to 29 percent of the education budget in 1981, and the total amount of local scholarships has been frozen at the 1978 level.

Nigeria. During the 1970s, the Federal Government withdrew from the allocation of bursaries in non-Federal universities and the responsibility was given to the state governments. It is not clear how effective this system is. What is clear is that the universities are increasing their incomes through the recent introduction of lodging and food charges (N468 a year) and the charging of fees for non-degree courses and post-graduate study. A period of national service is required for each graduate.

Senegal. All education is tuition free.

Sierra Leone. Tuition fees are charged by the universities but these are usually covered by central government scholarships and, increasingly, support provided by private industry. In 1985 lodging fees were substantially increased and the feeding subsidy withdrawn.

Somalia. All educational tuition costs plus board and lodging expenses are provided by the Government.

Sudan. Tuition and boarding are free. In 1976/77, student pocket money alone totalled more than book expenditures in Khartoum University and, overall, student welfare costs were 17.4 percent of the university's budget.

Swaziland. As is the case at all levels of education, university students have to contribute towards their education. Fees, charges and living expenses at the University in 1976 have been estimated at £680 while the average Government scholarship was £540. These scholarships have to be repaid within two years.

Tanzania. As in several other countries, a loan scheme was introduced in the early 1970s but was abolished due to the high costs of administration and presumed injustices. Loans were replaced by an obligation to work for the Government for five years. In addition to free tuition, students receive sh.500 (US $25) a month plus an annual book allowance of between sh.1000 and 3000 depending on the faculty. In 1982, the National Commission of Education recommended the reintroduction of a loan scheme but so far no action has been taken.

Uganda. No tuition fees are payable and each student receives 4800 shillings a year as pocket money.

Zambia. Tuition, board and food are provided free at the university. In addition, allowances are paid to all students.

In a paper by Mingat and Tan (1984) the extent of student subsidies in the Central African Republic, Congo, Niger and Togo are described. In none of these countries are tuition fees charged and allowances to cover living and other student related expenses are available for virtually all students.

From this survey a number of points stand out. First, apart from not altogether successful attempts in Lesotho and Swaziland, no government currently has a general policy of charging even partial tuition fees which are not then covered by some form of grant. Second, most governments bear the bulk of board and lodging expenses for most students. Third, a majority of governments provide allowances for additional living expenses. Fourth, a number of countries require either bonding to government employment or some period of national service on reduced income. In summary, virtually no African government charges tuition fees not covered by grants or requires most students to provide their own non-subsidised accommodation. In addition, probably a majority of governments also provide pocket money. Recent policies introduced in Sierra Leone, Nigeria and Malawi to reduce boarding subsidies, however, suggest that attitudes may be changing.

The arguments in favour of increasing student contributions to the cost of their education are based on a series of efficiency and equity considerations. These have been amply developed by, among others, Rogers (1972), Woodhall (1983), Mingat and Tan (1984) and Mingat and Psacharopoulos (1984) and are, therefore, only briefly presented below. On efficiency grounds it is argued that:

- demand for higher education would be high in developing countries even in the absence of subsidisation as a result of very high income benefits. These benefits constitute an economic rent for those few individuals who are able to gain access to a limited number of places. The existence of government subsidies increases these benefits. According to table 4.1, private rates of return to higher education in ten African countries average 32 percent compared to the average social return of 12 percent. Basically, it is argued that demand does not need to be stimulated by subsidisation and that in most countries a sufficient number of graduates would become available in its absence.

- a policy of charging students for tuition and/or living expenses would increase the incentives to students to make a more careful consideration of their educational options. Behind this supposition is the argument that the labour market transmits signals of shortages and surpluses through wages and levels and periods of unemployment which students would be more likely to give consideration to if their own level of investment in education was higher.

- increasing the economic contribution from students would improve their level of commitment to study, so reducing both repetition and dropout rates.

103

- the reduction in demand for higher education following an increase in the private contribution could result in a greater proportion of resources being used in primary and secondary education where, it is argued, social rates of return are greater.

The argument in favour of user charges based on equity considerations is that higher education leads to substantially higher earnings and therefore ought to be financed by those who gain. Even before their higher education courses, these students have enjoyed large amounts of public subsidy. Analyses of who pays and who benefits from higher education which have been made in developing countries (for instance, in Malaysia and Colombia) have shown that the present system of public subsidisation is highly regressive.

Given the very large differentials in earnings between higher education graduates and other workers, the high cost of this level of education and the obvious excess demand for it in most countries, it is difficult on the basis of economic theory to find strong arguments against the substitution of grants by loans. On the other hand, several of the 'efficiency' arguments put forward for loans are weak. Since large earnings premiums exist for all branches of higher education, it is not clear that with an increased private cost students would alter their subject choice acting more as 'investors' than 'consumers'. Given their secondary school qualifications, students appear to already opt first for subjects with the most lucrative career prospects. Again, there is no proven connection between lower repetition and dropout rates and increased private financing. For instance, these rates are extremely low in the United Kingdom where student subsidies are among the highest in the world. The argument that fees and charges would lower student demand, thereby releasing resources for educational levels with higher rates of return is also based on a very weak factual base. Many reasons exist to suspect that social returns calculated for African countries have been systematically biased upwards for primary schooling and downwards for higher education. The argument also presumes a budgetary system in which the total education budget is first decided and then divided between levels. Probably more common is the practice of building the total education budget upward from its consti-tuent parts. There is no reason to believe that savings from higher education would be directed towards primary schooling under such a system of budgeting.

The arguments in favour of greater student contributions which are based on considerations of equity appear much stronger. Earnings premiums are very sub-

104

stantial and public subsidisation is almost certainly highly regressive. However, under a scheme to simply increase charges or lower/abolish grants, it is likely that access to higher education places would become more restricted according to parental income unless a means-tested scholarship programme accompanied the scheme. With a comprehensive system of loans, however, the access argument against cost recovery disappears. If all students are offered loans which are paid back during working life there is no reason why this would have any significant effect on the ability of students from poor backgrounds to continue their studies. Loan schemes, however, which covered both tuition and accommodation would, in their initial period, use greater government resources than a policy which provided free tuition but required students to meet all their own living expenses.

The arguments generally made against increasing students' contributions are of two types – the political and the practical. A recent example of the first was in Nigeria in 1984 when student leaders were resisting increased charges in accommodation and food by pointing to the issue of redesigned army uniforms at a cost of $9.5 million. This type of argument has been used several times across both East and West Africa and has almost always resulted in generating sufficient opposition that governments have backed down. Another common argument is that simply by working at skilled jobs, students are repaying society. Examples of this attitude taken from a student panel discussion (Lauglo 1981) are:

Graduates are in fact repaying society through their work. It is a contribution to society when doctors cure illness, engineers build roads and bridges and teachers impart knowledge and skills to their students (Pakistani student).
Even if a person is highly paid, if a doctor saves one life then I think he has paid back what the government has given him (Tongan student).
If graduates remain in the country and work they are in fact contributing to the economy...therefore they are in fact repaying society (Zambian student).
In what sense is university really a privilege? There is very stiff competition to gain access to university. It is earned by ability and hard work (Kenyan student).

While graduates in many African countries have accepted the idea of national service schemes on reduced salary, actual repayment of part of the costs of higher education continues to be viewed in a hostile way.

Turning now to the feasibility of schemes to raise the student contribution to the costs of higher education, Woodhall (1983) points out in her comprehensive treatment of the whole student loans issue that an argument which has often been made against loans is that the amount which can be expected to be recouped is relatively small and, in any case, in no way provides a short term solution to financial constraints. In an attempt to quantitatively assess these arguments two simulation exercises have recently been made within the World Bank for African countries focussing on the size of student subsidies and their opportunity cost and the potential level of cost recovery. The first of these concentrated on the trade-off between subsidies for higher education students and places in primary schools (Mingat and Tan 1984) and the second on the degree of cost recovery feasible in different country groups under various assumptions of the proportion of incomes recouped (Mingat, Tan, Hoque 1984).

Using data from eight Francophone and two Anglophone African countries, the first set of simulations showed that a 50 percent cut in student living allowances (in kind or cash) could result in savings sufficient to fund a 10 percent increase in primary places. The second simulation was based essentially on data from Malawi but then generalised through data from the same set of countries described above. The aim of the study was to enquire what proportion of total unit costs in higher education could be reclaimed at different repayment rates.

The results of such an exercise depend essentially on the ratio of costs to earnings. Initial assumptions were that a rate of interest of 5 percent was charged and repayment was over ten years. For Malawi, an annual repayment equal to 10 percent of income would result in a rate of cost recovery of 16 percent. Repayments of 15, 20 and 25 percent of income would result in the recovery of 24, 32 and 39 percent of costs respectively. The authors conclude that it would be quite difficult to achieve a substantial rate of cost recovery in Malawi via loan schemes. Turning to the eight Francophone countries, however, the scheme appears more feasible as a result of higher graduate earnings. An annual repayment equal to 10 percent of salary over ten years would result in a rate of cost recovery of 64 percent and if the repayment was 15 percent, the recovery would be complete.

These sets of results lead back to the consideration of earnings differentials presented in chapter 4. There it was shown that, at least in several Anglophone countries, differentials attributable to higher education have been falling over time and in countries such as Ghana are now quite narrow. The smaller the differential, the weaker are both the efficiency and equity arguments for cost recovery schemes and the lower the feasibility of recovering a substantial proportion of costs. Similarly, the easier it is to absorb graduates into employment. The history of failure in introducing loan schemes in Africa and, where they have been introduced, of recouping significant payments has to be recognised. The likely increased pressure on governments to guarantee employment after graduation and to maintain earnings differentials following a loans scheme must also be considered. As a result, in countries where differentials are low emphasis is perhaps best placed on imposing charges for accommodation and ensuring that wage policies are implemented to continue the erosion of differentials. In this way, financial pressure on governments is eased both in terms of the education budget and its total wage bill together with the possibility of achieving a greater intensity of graduate employment throughout the economy.

Where, because of market pressures or for political reasons earnings differentials attributable to higher education are unlikely to fall, greater emphasis needs to be placed on designing loan schemes. This would appear to be the case for several Francophone West African countries and for the small countries in southern Africa. Alternatives to a loan scheme in these countries is a graduate tax and bonding or compulsory community service for a number of years at low pay. A graduate tax has the advantage over a loans scheme in that it affects all graduates thereby being more equitable. A potential disadvantage is the increased size of the pressure group threatened and the greater likelihood of increased wage demands. Bonding schemes with periods of community service on low pay already exist. These potentially reduce the government's wage bill but the costs of administration and provision of accommodation have, in practice, quite severely reduced the savings.

The experience over the last 15 years in African countries of failed attempts to implement loan schemes or introduce full cost charges for accommodation indicates the political problems involved. Examples of successful schemes in other parts of the world, such as Latin America, however, indicate that they are possible to implement. In African countries, the resolve of governments to ensure that students' contributions rise is likely to harden as the financial crisis is prolonged. Similarly, students' will to resist as the employment market tightens can also be expected to strengthen. Recent moves in Sierra Leone, Nigeria and Malawi to increase charges indicate that user cost measures are beginning to gain momentum.

8 University development and finance in West Africa

INTRODUCTION

Past chapters have surveyed the origins, development and costs of African universities in general terms. In this chapter, the analysis is more detailed and focusses on the universities of just two countries. The university systems of Ghana and Nigeria provide both comparable and contrasting experiences of higher education in Africa. In both countries, single universities were established in the late 1940s with a strong British influence over purpose, structure, curriculum, autonomy, standards, staffing and so on. As a result, by Independence, both countries had a university of international repute though there were those who argued that this had been achieved at high financial cost and at the expense of structures and curricula more appropriate to local circumstances.

During the 1960s, the number of universities increased to three in Ghana and five in Nigeria. Since then, however, there have been variations between the two countries in terms of the further expansion of institutions and enrolments and levels of government financing. In Ghana, no additional universities have opened and enrolments grew from 7179 in 1975 to just 8008 in 1984. In contrast, enrolments in Nigeria grew from 32,286 to 106,331 over the same period and by 1984 there were 17 federal and six state universities. Alongside these differences in rates of expansion, while economic stagnation and declining government revenues have led to a reduction in the level of university financing in Ghana, particularly over the past few years, in Nigeria economic optimism through much of the 1970s significantly bolstered all levels of the educational system. More recently, however, government revenues in Nigeria have also been falling and allocations to the universities are currently well below previous levels.

The universities in both Ghana and Nigeria are now under strong pressure to operate with lower levels of government resources than they were designed to use. As was emphasised in chapter 6, in order to begin to consider the implications for universities of financial constraints and the most appropriate and least damaging responses to these, disaggregated cost analyses are required. Such analyses, however, and any recommendations which result need to be grounded in some understanding of the universities' origins which have so deeply shaped the perceptions of all involved. Consequently, prior to the case studies which concentrate largely on the present financial position of universities in Ghana and Nigeria a short account of these origins, and some implications, is offered below.

Both the Asquith and Elliot Commissions which reported to the British government in 1945 supported the establishment of institutions of higher education in Africa and the Caribbean. Between 1945 and 1948, university colleges linked to the University of London were established in the Gold Coast, Nigeria, Sudan, Uganda and the West Indies. Essentially, the models for these institutions in terms of purpose and structure were British universities: 'In constitution, they were autonomous, deliberately detached from the state. In standards and curriculum they emphasised the thin stream of excellence and narrow specialism. In social function, they regarded themselves as restricted to an elite' (Ashby 1964, pp.11-12).

In 1948 the university colleges of Ibadan and the Gold Coast (at Legon) opened and enrolled 104 and 90 students respectively. The envisaged purpose and structure of both these university colleges required the development of a detached and self sufficient community and consequently both were located several miles outside existing towns. As Ashby again points out, this had substantial implications for the pioneer administrators. Not only did they have to establish a university but also provide roads, homes for staff, halls for students, drainage, water supplies, electricity, transport services, schools and even a cemetery. The development of self contained communities inevitably led to charges that these university colleges were 'ivory towers', divorced from the mass of the population and power bases insufficiently receptive to government needs (Austin 1976). In addition, maintenance of the infrastructure required was, and has continued to be, a major source of financial problems and misunderstandings. In a statement which would be fully understood by today's university administrators Mellanby, the first vice chancellor of Ibadan, wrote in 1958, 'It is salutory to realize that the expenditure in 1956/7 by University College, Ibadan on the single item "maintenance of grounds and buildings" was more than allowed by the

110

Elliot Commission for the entire annual cost of the University College' (p.12). Actual expenditures just four years after opening were over double those forecast, almost all the overrun being due to various forms of maintenance and travel.

The university colleges in sub Saharan Africa began as expensive institutions in relation to domestic resources. While Britain in 1956 had 85,000 students and Nigeria had 563, the cost in Britain represented 0.5 percent of government expenditure and in Nigeria, 2.0 percent (Mellanby 1958, p.11). Despite the existence of a few critics at the time, however, there appears to have been a sense of the inevitability of the high cost of universities if African countries were to establish institutions capable of producing a leadership equipped for self government and independence. The essence of the requirements of a university to achieve this goal is evocatively described by Austin (1985a) reminiscing about the University College of the Gold Coast in the 1950s.

> To dine there was memorable. The warm, tropical night, scented with frangipani, conjured away any disbelief there might be to the utility of a Cambridge college system which had taken flight to West Africa from the chilly fens of East Anglia. It had its courtyard, fountains, convocation tower, faculty buildings and library of white stone and red tiled roofs – Nuffield College among the hibiscus and bougainvillea. The appearance was truly magnificent and the reality was held to match the image (p.1910).

There was, then, seen to be one universal standard (a gold standard in Ashby's phrase) for university education and this standard implied a particular physical environment and level of services. These, in turn, were not generally available to the population of African societies, as in Europe, and therefore had to be provided to the few by the universities themselves.

The university colleges at Legon and Ibadan lay the base for higher education in Ghana and Nigeria. While some of the subsequent institutions have differed in detail, their purposes, expectations and operations have been largely similar. Today the universities in these countries face a financial crisis and, at least in Ghana, morale is extremely low and relations with government poor. In the two case studies which follow the, mainly financial, conditions of the universities in Ghana and Nigeria are described. The attempt is made to increase the understanding of the structure of university financing in

Africa and to demonstrate both the constraints to, and
opportunities for, altering this structure.

GHANA

Since the University of Ghana (previously the University
College of the Gold Coast) at Legon received its charter
and independence from the University of London in 1961,
two more universities have been created in Ghana – the
University of Science and Technology at Kumasi (again in
1961) and the University of Cape Coast (in 1971 after being
founded as a university college in 1961).   Both campus'
were established with facilities similar to those at Legon –
on a vast acreage outside of town with staff housing,
student halls, clinic, school, vehicle pool and the full
range of public services.   Both universities have also
followed similar ideals and adopted the same basic
organisational form as at the University of Ghana.
        The wide measure of legal autonomy allowed to the
universities, following the British model, in the context of
almost continual reciprocal suspicions between them and
successive governments has resulted in a lack of continuity
concerning their status.   At various times governments
have disestablished departments and institutes without
reference to academic boards, directly made appointments
to headships of departments, attempted to abolish
sabbatical leave, dismissed lecturers and professors
through the radio and closed the universities several times
(Austin 1985b).
        Again following the British pattern and based on the
University Grants Committee, a National Council of Higher
Education has twice been established (1962–66 and 1972–82)
to act as a co-ordinator of the universities and a buffer
between them and the government.   One of the Council's
major roles was in finance.   Universities submitted their
budgets to it and an internal hearing was held.   The
revised estimates were then presented and defended by the
Council in the 'external' hearings with the Ministry of
Finance.   Another role was to consider and give advice on
plans for the development of new university departments
and programmes.   Since the abolition of the Council in 1982
and the removal of its representatives from university
councils, a body to both represent and shield the
universities from government no longer exists.   Whatever
the instrument used and whatever the level of university
funding, there is again a need to rationalise the
procedures of budgeting and the release of funds. Although
detailed annual estimates continue to be prepared by the
universities, over the past two years block allocations to

112

them have simply been made monthly, and in arrears.

Part of the confusion which surrounds current financing procedures for the universities results from the general crisis in government finance. In the next section, this crisis is briefly documented together with evidence that the educational sector has taken a greater than average share of the consequences. Following this, trends in university enrolments since 1970 and some characteristics of the student population are described before total and unit costs of the sector are shown over time and disaggregated according to their various components. This part of the case study uses comparable data for a British university to underline the necessity for such disaggregation if false and potentially dangerous conclusions are not to be drawn from the global figures. In the final section, some of the steps which have already been taken to improve the financial health of the universities are described and further suggestions made.

Educational Finance

The present crisis in university financing in Ghana has to be seen in a wider economic and financial context. Basically, the recent economic performance of the economy has been poor. Over the past 15 years, gross domestic product (GDP) has remained virtually constant in real terms while per capita product has fallen substantially. Equally serious for the social services, government expenditure as a proportion of this constant GDP has systematically fallen, apart from a brief period in the mid 1970s, from 22 percent in 1970 to only 9 percent in 1984. For most of the 1970s combined recurrent and development expenditures on education as a share of this falling total government expenditure remained constant at around 20-22 percent. In the first half of the 1980s, however, they fell to an average of 17 percent and to just 14 percent in 1984. In sum, educational expenditure has fallen as a proportion of total government expenditure which itself has fallen as a proportion of a stagnant GDP. In absolute terms, out of every 100 cedis of national income, 4 cedis were spent on education in 1970, 3.6 cedis in 1979 and under 2 cedis in 1984. Since income has not grown in real terms, the absolute real level of government resources provided for education has fallen and most dramatically since 1979. Educational expenditures in 1984 were only between 30 and 40 percent of their real 1979 value. The situation is described fully in table 8.1.

One consequence of the reduced level of funding in recent years has been the almost stationary set of

Table 8.1. Education Expenditure Total Government Expenditure and GDP, Ghana.[a] (percent)

	1970	1973	1976	1979	1980	1981	1982	1983	1984
1. Total Government Expenditure % GDP	22	21	30	17	18	13	10	8	9
2. Recurrent Education Expenditure % Total Government Rec. Exp.	24	24	24	24	20	20	21	16	16
3. Total Education Expenditure % Total Government Expenditure	20	20	21	22	17	19	20	16	14
4. Total Education Expenditure % GDP	4.0	4.2	6.4	3.6	3.1	2.3	2.0	1.2	1.4

Notes: [a] From 1979 the totals are all preliminary figures.

Sources: World Bank (1984e), Ghana Ministry of Finance (1982a) and Ministry estimates.

enrolments at all levels of the educational system. Between 1981 and 1984 primary enrolments rose by an annual average of 1.5 percent, middle school enrolments by 1.1 percent and secondary school enrolments by 1.6 percent – rates all well below the increases in the relevant age groups leading to reduced enrolment ratios. In the universities, enrolments were actually lower in 1984 than in 1979; 8008 and 8288 respectively. Another consequence of reduced funding is a substantial decline in the real value of teachers' and lecturers' salaries and the virtual non existence of up to date teaching aids including books.

The constraints on government expenditure, made worse by substantial increases in resources required to service debts (up from 15 percent of total expenditures in 1980 to 27 percent in 1982) are highlighting in an extreme form an ambiguity common to universities across several African countries. That is, their apparent simultaneous under- and overfinancing. As will be described in the following pages, evidence of university underfinancing in Ghana is very obvious in libraries, laboratories, restrictions on field work, written materials, space, maintenance and so on. Also their absolute costs are well below those in most other African countries. Overfinancing, however, is claimed by those who compare the universities' unit costs with those of other educational institutions and find they are 16 times higher than for secondary schools and over 70 times higher than for primary schools. A sympathetic observer of the universities has described the situation in the following way, 'One might well call the provision of university finance generous if it were not the case that all three universities are unable to teach adequately or to undertake research at past levels of commitment' (Austin 1985b, p.1864). Attempting to irradicate this apparent ambiguity by equipping universities to produce quality teaching in relevant disciplines while holding constant or reducing government funded unit costs is the main issue facing both the university community and the government. Before this issue is directly faced, the section below describes the growth and levels of enrolments and some of the characteristics of the university students.

University Students

Enrolments in Ghanaian universities were 790 in 1961, 4731 in 1970 and 8008 in 1984. Rates of growth have varied considerably over different time periods. Between 1961 and 1970, enrolments grew substantially in all universities at an overall annual average of 22 percent. Between 1970 and 1975 the growth rate slowed to 10 percent and then to just

2 percent up to 1980. Since then there has been virtually no growth. In fact enrolments in 1984 were below those in 1979. Table 8.2 presents enrolments in each university for selected years between 1970 and 1984.

Table 8.2. University Enrolments 1970–1984, Ghana

	1970/71	1975/76	1980/81	1984/85
University of Ghana	2,525	3,620	3,881	3,352
University of Cape Coast	862	1,205	1,405	1,568
University of Science and Technology	1,344	2,354	3,002	3,088
Total	4,731	7,179	7,951	8,008
Annual Average Growth (%)		10.3	2.2	0.2

Source: University of Ghana (1985).
        University of Cape Coast (1982) and (1984).
        University of Science and Technology (1985).

Before the reasons for the stagnation in enrolments are discussed, some additional information is available on the characteristics of the student body. First, it is almost entirely an undergraduate population. At Cape Coast, 4.7 percent of students are postgraduates and at Legon, 5.1 percent. These figures are below those for 1970, and for 1976 it is reported that 18 percent of students were postgraduate. In a period of financial squeeze, emphasis has clearly been placed on undergraduates. Another very evident characteristic of the student body is that it is male dominated. In 1984, female students constituted 17.5 percent of all enrolments at Legon and 19.1 percent at Cape Coast. These proportions have grown only slowly since 1970 when 11 and 14 percent of the students at these two universities were women. Students can also be differentiated by social background. No recent analysis of this characteristic has been made but Weiss (1981) has compiled studies of the occupational distribution of students' fathers made in 1951–3, 1962 and 1974. The results are reproduced in table 8.3. According to these data, the trends observable between 1951–3 and 1963   of an

116

Table 8.3. Occupational Distribution of Male Students' Fathers or Guardians in All Ghanaian Universities

Father's Occupation	1951–53		1962–63		1974	
	Percentage	Number	Percentage	Number	Percentage	Number
Higher professional, higher commercial	16.4	63	8.6	27	9.0	119
Lower professional	17.2	66	9.9	31	28.5	375
Clerical	12.8	49	10.5	33	5.1	67
Lower commercial	16.2	62	13.7	43	10.1	133
Craft, manual	8.4	32	11.5	36	11.1	146
Farming, fishing	29.0	111	45.9	144	36.2	476
Total	100.0	383	100.0	314	100.0	1,316

Source: L. Weiss (1981) p.25.

117

increased social openness of the universities were reversed in the following decade. In 1951-3, over 33 percent of students' fathers had professional or semi-professional occupations while the corresponding figure in 1963 was 18 percent. Over the same period, children of manual workers and farmers increased from 37 percent to 57 percent. Between 1963 and 1974, however, an opposite movement occurred with the children of professional and semi-professional men increasing from 18 to 27 percent and of manual and farming men decreasing from 57 to 47 percent. With the expansion of places having slowed down substantially since 1974, it can be assumed that an even greater proportion of places are today filled by children with professional and semi-professional backgrounds.

The level of enrolments in the universities is left to the university authorities to decide. No guidance is given by government and no plan for manpower development exists. Occasionally, courses are added at the request of individual ministries, for instance for health inspectors, and of professional associations, for example in book production. According to senior administrators in each university, the major constraint on enrolment expansion is student boarding facilities. At each, non-residential students have been registered but the non-availability of rooms for renting in Accra, Kumasi and Cape Coast at prices affordable and the almost complete lack of transport facilities between the towns and the universities over the past few years have simply led to multiple occupation of halls of residence rooms. For instance, the University of Science and Technology now sets a maximum of three persons in rooms designed for single occupancy though even this is known to be often exceeded. At Cape Coast, halls of residence have stood half finished for several years and attempts by all three universities to interest the private sector in building and renting student accommodation have had no success. It appears to be clear that, however funded, without additional student accommodation university enrolments cannot increase.

If university places do not increase, enrolment ratios and the chances of secondary school graduates furthering their education will decrease. Over the last few years, enrolments in secondary sixth forms have been increasing at an annual rate of 4.5 percent and currently 52 percent of leavers find university places. Table 8.4 shows the numbers of applicants and acceptances for 1985 entry to the University of Science and Technology. Since students have to apply to the universities separately, these figures for a single university do not provide an accurate picture of excess demand. They do provide some information, however,

118

Table 8.4. Applications and Enrolments by Department
           University of Science and Technology, Ghana, 1985

	Qualified Applicants	Enrolled	Percentage Enrolled
Agriculture	220	81	37
Architecture	102	59	36
Art	108	72	67
Engineering	395	204	52
Pharmacy	224	45	20
Science	159	112	70
Social Science	1,104	155	14
Medical Science	172	40	23
Computing	325	50	15
Renewable Resources	80	40	50
Total	2,949	858	29

Note: 'Qualified' is defined as possession of two 'A'
      levels.

Source: University of Science and Technology mimeo.

and in particular demonstrate the relative degree of excess
demand between subjects. The variations in success rates
are very wide, ranging from 14 percent in the social
sciences to 70 percent in science. Data from the University
of Cape Coast are similar with acceptance rates for 1985
being 70 percent in science and 30 percent in education.
    The initial academic orientations of the universities
at Kumasi and Cape Coast were designed to avoid
duplication with the University of Ghana at Legon. As the
first university, the latter offered a broad range of
courses in the arts, social sciences and pure sciences.
Agriculture and medicine were added later. Between 1961
and 1970, 51 percent of graduates studied Arts, 21 percent
Law, Economics and Administration and 25 percent Science,
Medicine and Agriculture. To compensate for what was
regarded as a major omission, Kumasi was established to
deal mainly with science and technology and Cape Coast
was originally named the University College of Science
Education. Over time the authorities at Kumasi have
replaced what was originally a liberal arts department

119

having a servicing function by a fully fledged social
science faculty and a medical school was also added,
controversially, in the mid 1970s. When Cape Coast
graduated to a fully fledged university in 1971, the
emphasis on science teaching alone was dropped. Today
there are faculties of Arts, Social Studies, Science and
Education. This process of delimitation of function was
defended by Professor Dickson, currently vice-chancellor of
Cape Coast, several years ago (Dickson 1973, p.108) on
educational grounds. However, when it occurs in those
subjects with the highest unit costs where economies of
scale might be most expected, as in agriculture and
medicine, the economics are also important. These are
described later. Table 8.5 presents data on enrolments in
degree subjects by university for 1984.

Table 8.5. Distribution of University Enrolments by Subject
            1984/85, Ghana

Area of Study	University of Ghana	University of Cape Coast	University of Science & Technology
Arts	1,534	492	–
Social Studies		474	480
Science	324	292	640
Agriculture	139	97	256
Medicine	316		171
Administration	352		
Education		209	
Engineering			779
Architecture			298
Pharmacy			163
Art			208

Source: University sources.

University Finance
     Analysing the financial structure of higher education
in Ghana is not straightforward. The most recent complete
set of fully audited accounts for the individual
universities' recurrent expenditures are for 1979-80.
Detailed estimates of actual expenditures are available for
each university since that date up to 1983 but not for the
same year. In addition, on the basis of the monthly block

grants allocated to the universities approximations of total expenditures can be made for financial years 1984 and 1985. Actual expenditures of the primary and secondary education cycles are available for 1979 and 1984, as are the government's final estimates for 1985. All these data are presented in table 8.6 together with estimations of the proportion of total recurrent educational expenditures devoted to the universities.

Table 8.6. Recurrent Financing of Basic, Secondary and University Education Selected Years, Ghana (cedi, '000)

	1979/80	1984	1985
University of Ghana	45,068	186,000	320,000
University of Cape Coast	30,157	120,000	207,000
University of Science & Technology	37,596	180,000	344,000
Total University	112,821	486,000	871,000
Basic & Secondary Cycle	798,821	3,233,000	6,795,000
Total Recurrent Education Expenditure	910,980	3,714,000	7,666,000
University Recurrent as % of Total Educational Recurrent	12.4	13.0	11.3

Notes and Sources: University expenditure:
1979/80 Final Audited Reports
1984 University of Ghana – actual expenditure from estimates. University of Cape Coast and University of Science & Technology – estimations
1985 Actual to October plus estimates to end of year

Basic & Secondary expenditure:
1979 Ministry of Finance (1982a)
1984 Actual expenditure, Government Education Service
1985 Final Estimates, Ministry of Finance

121

From the description of the data underlying table 8.6 it is apparent that not all the figures can be relied upon. The best estimate, however, is that the universities and their teaching departments currently consume around 12 percent of total recurrent education expenditure and that this proportion has varied little over the past few years. The fall in the real value of total education expenditure has been previously described. The universities, then, have been receiving a constant proportion of a declining total.

The real starting point for debates on the under- or overfinancing of university education is the cost per student per year - the unit cost. Before estimates of these are presented, two qualifications need to be made. Unit costs of students in universities are typically calculated on the basis of total expenditures implying that all resources are devoted to teaching. In fact, the teaching function in most universities is meant to be only one of several functions with graduates only one of several outputs. Another major function is research. To the extent that faculty spend time on research and use university facilities, the costs involved should be subtracted from total costs. Since it is impossible to value the costs and benefits of research in the Ghanaian universities no allowance is made for them in the calculations of unit costs. However, it is useful to be aware that the results of these calculations are at the upper limit. A second qualification concerns the conversions of university costs from cedis to United States dollars. While it is useful to provide some sort of international yardstick, in countries with overvalued currencies and exchange rates which have changed substantially over time, the yardstick must be handled carefully. In Ghana, for instance, between 1983 and 1986 the number of cedis to the dollar increased from 2.75 to 90.

With these qualifications in mind, table 8.7 presents estimates of unit costs by university for various years between 1979-80 and 1984-5. A number of conclusions can be drawn. First, the average unit cost over the three universities in 1984-85 was around $2000. This compares to a unit cost of $7000 in a typical, small, provincial British university in the same year (see below) and to an average of $4335 for 17 East African universities sampled in table 6.1. Second, unit costs were highest in both 1979-80 and 1984-85 at the university with lowest enrolments, Cape Coast, though by the latter date they were only 27 percent above the average. There is, then, some evidence of increasing returns to scale. Third, despite the Universities of Ghana and Science and Technology teaching distinctly

Table 6.7. Unit Costs of University Students, by University, Ghana

University	Academic Year				
	1979/80	1980/81	1981/82	1982/83	1984/85
Ghana					
Students	3,881			3,384	3,352
Allocation ('000)	45,070			124,860	320,000
Unit Cost (¢)	11,612			36,897	95,465
Unit Cost ($)	4,225			1,475	1,801
Cape Coast					
Students	1,405	1,430			1,568
Allocation ('000)	30,160	4,243			207,000
Unit Cost (¢)	21,464	29,670			132,000
Unit Cost ($)	7,805	10,790			2,490
Science and Technology					
Students	3,002		2,726		3,088
Allocation ('000)	37,600		61,900		344,000
Unit Cost (¢)	12,525		22,707		111,560
Unit Cost (4)	4,550		8,257		2,105
Overall Unit Cost (¢)	13,613				108,756
($)	4,950				2,052
Exchange Rate ¢:$	2.75	2.75	2.75	25	53
Price Index	100				1237

Sources: 1979/80, 1980/81, 1981/82, 1982/83 are actual expenditures taken from the individual universities' balance sheets and accounts. 1984/85 expenditures are allocations made through 1985.

different sets of courses, unit costs appear very similar. Finally, the apparent reduction in average unit costs over the period from around $5000 to $2000 needs to be carefully considered since part of this results from substantial devaluations. On the basis of the official price index, it appears that in constant cedi prices, the average unit cost fell by around 35 percent.

So far, two financial calculations have been presented to illustrate the financial position of Ghanaian universities: first their share of total educational expenditure and second their unit costs. The following discussion questions whether these shares and costs can be regarded as too high or too low, whether current expenditures are efficiently made, whether there are possibilities of the government reducing its share of unit costs and the desirability and practicability of enrolment expansion.

Under- or Overfinanced Universities?

There are no objectively determined 'optimum' levels of funding for universities in the developed or less developed countries. In a number of areas, however, it is very obvious that Ghanaian universities are underfinanced and that the resulting quality of education is low. These areas are discussed in turn.

Teaching Staff. According to the universities, in October 1984 there was a total of 624 faculty at post and 721 vacancies. While the level of vacancies should be regarded with some scepticism and if filled would result in extremely low student:faculty ratios there does appear to be some understaffing and in some departments the situation is critical. At the University of Ghana there is one member of teaching staff in computing, one in statistics, one in philosophy and two in mathematics. At the medical school in Kumasi, three quarters of established posts are vacant. Staffing levels have not always been so low. They fell by one third at Cape Coast between 1981 and 1983 and by one fifth at Legon between 1978 and 1983. The use which currently has to be made of working professionals as well as staff from the other universities, while a useful development in certain respects, makes coherent teaching programmes difficult to create. The low staffing levels are not a direct consequence of a lack of finance for existing salary levels. They result from more remunerative opportunities for employment in Nigeria and Liberia and from what are perceived to be deteriorating conditions of work. The latter include the lack of books, periodicals, equipment, research funds and conference

124

funds resulting in a general feeling by faculty that they are totally isolated from developments in their field taking place in other parts of the world.

Libraries. The libraries in each university are over-utilised for both teaching and research. The situation at the University of Science and Technology is indicative of the general situation. For 3088 students, there are 60 reading spaces in the undergraduate library and 40 in the reference library. Prior to 1979, the libraries had built up stocks of 160,000 books and subscribed to 583 periodicals. Since then all subscriptions have lapsed and no books have been purchased. At the same time neither faculty nor students can afford to make their own purchases and no photocopying facilities are available.

Equipment. The lack of equipment and inappropriateness of much which exists is naturally greatest in science and technology. The University of Science and Technology again provides examples. The last time equipment was purchased for the electrical engineering department was in 1962 and for civil engineering most dates from the 1950s. While computer work is regarded as essential across faculties, the existing computer is old, expensive to maintain and is only rarely operative. At the University of Ghana, a report from the faculty of science documents shortages of chemicals and other consumables necessary for the running of laboratory classes and claims that overseas orders are never supplied because of foreign exchange difficulties.

Services. The universities are located outside of towns. Without vehicles their administration is hampered in several ways. Similarly, without transport there can be no student fieldtrips and little experimental or data based research. Another service now broken down and unrepaired for lack of spare parts is the telephone system.

Physical Facilities. All the universities have unfinished buildings on which work has virtually been suspended. No allocations for capital works have been made since 1981. At Kumasi there is an incomplete library extension and central teaching block and at Cape Coast a library, halls of residence and teaching blocks all lie unfinished. At present, while there are differences between departments and subjects, teaching rooms are said to be overcrowded and to provide an absolute constraint to enrolment expansion. The other constraint, already mentioned, is student accommodation. Overcrowding is general and, among other drawbacks, provides problems for services such as water supplies and sewerage systems designed for half or a third of the actual inhabitants.

There can be no doubt that many aspects of university education in Ghana are presently underfinanced and are hampering effective teaching and research. Looked at from the primary and secondary schools, however, and from a government which faces demands for resources from many other activities the universities may still appear privileged. The universities consume around 12 percent of total educational expenditures yet teach under one percent of all pupils and 0.7 percent of the relevant age-group. Students spend their lives in halls of residence, served by porters, waiters, cooks and cleaners for which there is no charge. The grounds of the universities are large and landscaped with flowerbeds and exotic trees and maintained by a large workforce. For the staff, medical facilities, vehicle loans and allowances, schooling and substantial housing and pensions are all provided at very little cost. Until recently, air fares to Europe were provided for sabbatical leave. All these aspects of university life, and many others, are well beyond the experiences of virtually any other section of the population. In this context, the universities' pleas of poverty may be treated sceptically. And even more so when their government-financed unit costs are compared to those at other levels of education. Table 8.8 presents such a comparison. In very basic terms, the annual costs of educating one student at university is the same as educating 16 pupils at secondary school and 75 students at primary school. These comparisons provide a strong base for arguments that government financed unit costs at the universities are too high.

Table 8.8. Approximate Unit Costs by Level of Education, 1984 Ghana (cedis)

Level	Unit Cost
Primary	903
Middle	1274
Secondary	4303
Teacher Training	16020
Technical Institute	11790
University	67554

Source: Government Education Service.

Two sets of evidence have been presented to show that it could be argued that Ghanaian universities are both under- and overfinanced. As a result, it is important to analyse the costs further and, in particular, to divide them into their various components. This is attempted in the following section.

Composition of Unit Costs

To highlight some of the important and peculiar features of the cost structures of the Ghanaian universities, comparisons are made throughout this section with a British university of similar size and age - the University of East Anglia (UEA) which has around 4000 students and was established in the mid 1960s on the outskirts of a city. Table 8.9 presents a breakdown of university expenditures by activity. Categorisation of the multitude of headings covered in the universities' accounts into eight activities (including 'other') obviously necessitates a degree of arbitrariness and individual percentage figures should be treated with care. Because of this and to ease comparisons, the percentages for the three Ghanaian universities have also been averaged for each activity.

Differences in the proportions of total expenditures allocated between activities in the Ghanaian universities and the British one are clearly substantial. The outstanding difference is the proportion of total expenditure allocated to academic departments for salaries, materials and other running costs. In the British university this is 63 percent and in the Ghanaian universities, 23.5 percent. Adding expenditures for libraries further increases the difference. Conversely, expenditures on the maintenance of premises are 15 and 35 percent and on health services 1 and 11 percent respectively. In absolute terms, while total unit costs are around three and a half times greater in the British university than in the Ghanaian ones ($7000 and $2000), direct teaching costs are nine times greater ($4400 and $470).

The size of non-direct teaching expenditures in the Ghanaian universities results largely from decisions made about the roles of the university and the environment required to support these, made in the late 1940s at Legon and repeated in the early 1960s at Kumasi and Cape Coast. As was emphasised in the introduction to this chapter, Ghanaian universities were designed as virtual townships and with a large degree of planned welfarism and subsidisation of services. The sites are enormous, resulting in extensive road, water, electricity, fire fighting and sewerage systems and in the necessity for large numbers of guards and groundsmen. Nurseries, schools and health services were provided from the

127

Table 8.9. Percentage Breakdown of Actual Expenditure: Ghanaian and British Universities

Item	UG 1983/84	UST 1981/82	UCC 1982/82	Average Ghana	UEA 1983/84
Academic Departments	23.3	33.0	14.6	23.5	62.9
Library	3.4	1.1	1.3	1.9	5.2
Staff and Student Facilities	9.8	10.0	15.2	11.7	3.8
Administration	14.8	11.1	14.0	13.2	7.2
Premises	30.6	33.5	40.0	34.6	14.6
Minor Works	2.7	2.4	2.9	2.7	2.3
Health	12.4	7.9	13.0	11.1	0.7
Other	3.0	1.0	0.0	1.3	3.3
	100.0	100.0	100.0	100.0	100.0

Notes: UG is University of Ghana, UST is University of Science and Technology, UCC is University of Cape Coast, UEA is University of East Anglia.

Source: Ghanaian universities: Annual Recurrent Estimates (various years). University of East Anglia (1984a).

beginning together with substantial housing at low rents and with free maintenance. Being outside the towns, large fleets of vehicles have been necessary and become the norm (or now, the expectation). Simply because of the way in which the universities were originally regarded and designed, a relatively large amount of resources is now necessary to maintain them, even at the most minimum standard, before any teaching costs are incurred. This fact places an enormous constraint on efforts to reduce university costs without reducing teaching costs and quality.

Another way of diagnosing expenditures is by item. In the British university, personal emoluments accounted for 75 percent of total expenditures in 1984. At the University of Ghana in 1983 this proportion was 42 percent and at the University of Science and Technology it was 53 percent in 1981-82 and 68 percent in 1985. The greater proportion of wage costs in the British university reflects a higher ratio of wage level to other costs than in Ghana. It does not reflect higher staffing levels. These are presented in table 8.10 for each university and compared to student numbers.

As a result of the large exodus of university teaching staff from Ghanaian universities over the past few years, the overall student:teaching staff ratio has risen to 13.2:1, higher than the ratio in Britain. The teaching staff establishment, however, implies a ratio of only 6:1, well below European or North American norms. It is levels of non-teaching staff, however, in relation to both students and teaching staff which provide the greatest contrast. In the British university there are over six students to each member of the non-teaching staff; in Ghana, there are more staff than students! Similarly at the University of East Anglia there are 1.6 non-teaching staff per teacher; in Ghana there are 14.2. In financial terms, 55 percent of total staff costs at the University of East Anglia is for teachers compared to only 29 percent at the University of Ghana.

A comparison of the distribution of non-teaching staff among activities highlights the drain on resources resulting from the large infrastructure of Ghanaian universities. Table 8.11 provides this information for the Universities of Cape Coast and East Anglia. Considering the levels of enrolments, the numbers of non-teaching staff are much greater at Cape Coast in every activity. It is in the non-teaching and non-administration activities, however, that they are comparatively greatest. Enrolments at East Anglia are over two and a half times those at Cape Coast yet the staffing level for grounds, maintenance and

129

Table 8.10. University Student Staff Ratios at Ghanaian and British Universities, 1984

	UG	CC	UST	Ghana	UEA
Students	3,352	1,568	3,088	8,008	4,123
Teaching staff (at post)	251	94	260	605	410
Student:staff	13.3	16.7	11.9	13.2	10.1
Teaching staff establishment	481	277	587	1,345	410
Student:staff establishment	7.0	5.7	5.3	6.0	10.1
Non-teaching staff	3,214	2,213	3,155	8,582	658
Student:non-teaching staff	1.0	0.7	1.0	0.9	6.3
Non-teaching:teaching staff	12.8	23.5	12.1	14.2	1.6

Source: Students:table 8.2.
Teaching and non-teaching staff:university records.

Table 8.11. Employment of Non-Academic Staff by Selected
Activity Universities of Cape Coast and East Anglia

Activity	UCC 1982	UEA 1984
Departmental	272	223
Central Administration	161	99
Library	48	47
Hospital	105	17
Guards	238	44
Grounds	226	23
Maintenance	438	99
Enrolments	1,592	4,123

Source: UCC (1982).
           UEA (1984b).

security is less than one fifth.
        It has been argued so far that the non-academic
expenditures dominate the unit costs of Ghanaian
universities and that the greatest opportunities for cost
reduction lie in this area.   The pattern of course
offerings, however, also influences overall unit costs since
some subjects are more expensive than others.   Table 8.12
presents unit costs by subject at the University of Science
and Technology for 1981-82 and 1984-85 broken down into
departmental and common overhead costs.   Departmental
unit costs vary substantially but apart from agriculture
and pharmacy, the variations are largely swamped by the
common overhead costs.   The case of agriculture, however,
is important since all three universities offer the subject.
At the University of Ghana in 1983, the average
departmental unit cost was ₡6007 compared to ₡31,812 in
agriculture.   Teaching students agriculture at the
University of Science and Technology instead of, say,
social science, added ₡5 million in 1981-82 compared to a
total university expenditure of ₡67 million.
        The final aspect of costs to be discussed covers
student board and lodging and the issue of fees.   At
present, tuition and accommodation are totally free and the
government allocates ₡34 a day (1985) to cover the cost of
two meals (₡7616 a year).   For the Universities of Cape
Coast and Science and Technology it has been possible to
isolate those expenditures incurred in running and main-

131

Table 8.12. Unit Teaching Cost and Unit Total Cost by University Faculty, UST (cedis)

Faculty	Total Department Costs ('000)	Students	Department Unit Cost	Common Unit Cost	Total Unit Cost
1981/82					
Agriculture	6,038	298	20,261	15,040	35,301
Pharmacy	1,333	156	8,545	15,040	23,585
Architecture	2,332	307	7,596	15,040	22,636
Science	4,101	571	7,182	15,040	22,222
Engineering	3,585	685	5,233	15,040	20,247
Social Science	1,358	369	3,680	15,040	18,720

Source: University Estimates.

132

taining the halls of residence. These are shown, together with total food costs, in table 8.13. The figures indicate that accommodation and feeding costs constitute around 10 percent of total recurrent costs.

Table 8.13. Total and Per Student Cost of Board and Feeding at Universities of Cape Coast and Science and Technology, 1984/85 (cedis)

	Cape Coast	Science and Technology
Residences		
Emoluments	5,202,000	10,807,000
Recurrent	2,470,980	5,300,000
Feeding grant		
(¢34 a day)	11,942,000	23,518,000
Total Overall Cost	19,617,000	39,685,000
Students	1,568	3,088
Cost per student	12,509	12,851

Source: University Estimates.

Policy Implications of Cost Analysis

The universities in Ghana have not increased their enrolments since 1979. As secondary school enrolments have continued to expand, the result has been a fall in transition ratios to higher education. In addition, there are indications that the country is slowly beginning to move out of the economic stagnation of the past decade and that the demand for graduates will increase. The desirability of enrolment expansion, therefore, is a very real issue. In this context and given the government's general reluctance to increase its financial contribution to the universities a number of implications result from the cost analysis of the previous section.

Several areas of the universities operations have been shown to be underfinanced, resulting in low levels of efficiency. Overall, however, and when compared to other levels of education within the country unit costs are relatively high. The cause of this apparent ambiguity is the high level of running costs of the non-teaching services of the universities imposed by their original conception and design. Comparing the departmental unit costs with those of non-boarding secondary schools, the difference is fourfold rather than the sixteenfold implied by total costs.

133

The structure of costs has two implications. First, it has to be recognised that the operation of institutions in Africa which bear a reasonably strong resemblance, and reach standards equal, to institutions in Europe and North America will be expensive in terms of any form of domestic comparison. To achieve a similar end-product in African countries requires universities themselves to directly finance services which are provided out of other budgets or out of the higher incomes of individuals in industrialised countries. An example is health services. The exodus of teaching faculty to universities in Nigeria and Liberia also demonstrates that an international market exists for their labour and that without some minimum level of academic support, they will withdraw. The conclusion is harsh. Either the model of higher education so far adopted is fundamentally changed and the existing institutions are converted into some form of post-secondary schools offering two year, 45 week a year general degrees based on large lectures and single set texts or some acceptance of large overhead costs has to be made.

If the universities are to retain their current roles and structure and become more effective in achieving their educational functions while not increasing their share of government expenditure, there is another set of implications. This includes attempts to both concentrate more of their own funds on directly educational activities and increase non-government resources. In addition the implications of enrolment expansion need to be faced. Most of the rest of this section considers these issues. Initially, however, the measures already taken by the universities to reduce costs, adapt to lower levels of government funding and raise additional funds are discussed.

Several cost reduction measures have already been taken, from the withdrawal of air-fares for study leave to significant reductions in the numbers of junior staff employed. At the University of Ghana, for example, junior staff on permanent contracts decreased by 36 percent between 1981 and 1984 and there is a general willingness by the authorities to reduce staff further and contract work out to tender. In addition to a reduced wage bill, such action also relieves the universities of some responsibilities for housing, superannuation, medical treatment, transport and so on. Another attempt to reduce the demands on the universities' allocations has focussed on ensuring that service units become self financing. These include the bookshops and the photocopying, printing, construction and maintenance units.

The main source of additional non-government funds

is expected to be via the universities' commercialisation schemes. Although all three universities are making attempts along these lines, the University of Science and Technology has gone furthest. Activities include the manufacture and sale of beds, chairs, windows, soap, pumps and traffic lights, the rearing of cattle, fish and poultry, a 300 acre oil palm project and servicing of fridges, freezers, air conditioners and motors. While there are some problems with these schemes such as the raising of initial capital, acquiring small but essential amounts of foreign exchange and ensuring that they do not over-involve faculty to the detriment of teaching, early experiences suggest that their potential benefits may be significant. In several ways, then, the universities have already begun to adapt to a harsher financial climate. The previous discussion of the condition of the universities and the composition of unit costs suggests that further steps could be considered to reduce or shift costs alongside others which would directly strengthen the universities' operations.

To increase financial discipline, reduce the arbitrariness of allocations and develop greater dialogue between the universities and the government, sets of norms for staffing and other areas of funding need to be agreed upon. If these were along the lines set by the Nigerian National Universities Commission and outlined in the second case study, their likely effect would be a further reduction in non-teaching staff, a redistribution of teaching staff between faculties, a slight increase in departmental recurrent and research budgets and a larger increase in the allocation to libraries. Once the funding of teaching has been consolidated, attention could be focussed on the activities which make up the majority of the expenditures, particularly those directed to maintaining infrastructure. Almost 30 percent of all non salary expenditures at one of the universities in 1985 was spent on repairs and maintenance, 10 percent on furniture mainly for staff housing, a further 10 percent on electricity and water much of which is used in staff houses and student hostels and almost 10 percent on transport. There is a great deal of hidden subsidisation of staff and students involved in these expenditures. It would be helpful if this was made explicit so that decisions whether to continue in this way, increase charges, increase salaries, provide loans and so on could be made more rationally.

The question of fees, charges and loans for students is again being actively discussed in Ghana. Williams (1974) has described the failure of the first attempt to introduce loans in 1971 and the Ghana Commercial Bank has recently disclosed that it is owed ₵50 million by 27,000 graduates dating back to the introduction of a second scheme in 1975 (West Africa, 9 December, 1985). At present there are no tuition fees and the Government provides the university with an amount to cover two meals a day. In contrast, at secondary schools, boarding fees are ₵4620 a year.

At a public debate organised by the Ministry of Education in mid 1985 around these issues, the lecturers' union supported the introduction of fees together with a loan scheme for those unable to pay (Asante 1985). Opponents stressed the common arguments that loans made on commercial terms would impose impossible burdens on graduates while concessionary terms would make loans attractive to those who did not need them; that means tests would not be effective; that there would be no immediate savings; that such schemes divert attention away from more fundamental issues in the running of universities; that participation in the national service scheme would be less willing and that given the existing narrow earnings differentials graduates would end up with a lower level of earnings than those who did not attend university. Student union representatives were also less than enthusiastic about students joining other university groups in commercialisation and food production schemes.

Calculation of the boarding and feeding costs shown in table 8.13 allows a reasonably precise assessment of the requirements of a loan scheme to cover these costs. Over three years the total involved is around ₵38,000 and with the planned increase to ₵51 per student per day in the feeding grant to universities this will rise to around ₵50,000. Current gross starting salaries in the public service are ₵30,000 ($526) a year and show very little progression. At a discount rate of 10 percent, the loan to cover boarding and feeding costs would be repaid if 18 percent of gross annual income was claimed over a whole working lifetime. With present salary levels this would result in a negative differential for the university graduate yet would still only cover around 10 percent of total unit costs. Whether this level of recovery is worth the effort of establishing a scheme, plugging the holes caused by emigration and increasing the pressures to raise salaries and so on is doubtful. More feasible might be the abolition of the feeding subsidy followed by the introduction of boarding charges linked to a scheme whereby students would be offered manual work currently done by university employees or contractors.

Finally the question of enrolment expansion will have to be faced in the near future as both the economy's demands for educated labour and the number of sixth form leavers increases. Austin (1976) remarked that at Legon, the buildings had been designed for a student population of 1000 and that little had been done to add to them. Between 1962 and 1970 only two new permanent teaching blocks were completed and since then there have been no more. As previously described, all campus' have unfinished buildings. A study of the implications for capital costs, recurrent costs and additional students of completing these buildings is required. The major constraint on enrolment expansion, however, is accommodation. Experiments to substantially increase numbers of non-residential students in the past simply resulted in severe overcrowding in halls of residence not designed for multiple occupation. However, the cost per place of building new halls of residence on the pattern of previous ones has been estimated at $10,000-15,000. Clearly, new halls of this type cannot be afforded. The only feasible answer is to build dormitory accommodation as in the secondary schools and provide plenty of study areas. Existing halls could then be used by final year students. If this option is regarded as being too expensive or alternatively if it is rejected by students and their power is too great to ignore, then a system of double annual intake using two 24 week terms could be examined.

NIGERIA

For the second case study of university development and finance in sub Saharan Africa, the region's richest and most populous country, Nigeria, has been chosen. There, the number of institutions and enrolments and levels of finance have expanded considerably over the past 15 years to levels far higher than elsewhere. The result is that today, around one third of all the region's universities are located in Nigeria. Much of the expansion since the early 1970s has been financed by increased oil revenue. In the last few years, however, the demand for oil and its price have fallen. Falling government revenues leading to substantially reduced levels of funding for the universities is adding to the strains already experienced in the universities as a result of rapid expansion. This case study documents an example of considerable growth in the university sector in sub Saharan Africa. It also demonstrates the common financial weaknesses of the underlying financial structure of the sector and the educational consequences of this when resources are reduced.

University Development

In the introduction to the country case studies, some aspects of the first decade of university education in Nigeria were described. This period was dominated by the University College of Ibadan which until 1960 was the only university level institution in the country. The college reflected the humanistic side of British higher education. While by the late 1950s there were no courses in engineering, economics, law, geology, anthropology or public administration, instruction was provided in Latin, Greek and ancient history (Ashby 1964, p.57). Other structural, constitutional and physical aspects of the college have already been mentioned sufficiently to convey the impression of an institution of high standard but rather remote, elite and expensive.

In 1960 a second university, the University of Nigeria, was established at Nsukka in the Eastern Region. The design of the academic structure of this university differed substantially from Ibadan in that it was fashioned after the land grant colleges of the United States and had very strong contacts with Michigan State University. Admission requirements were liberalised, course unit and evaluation procedures introduced and a wide range of courses with directly vocational orientations was offered.

Also, 1960 was the year when a commission, chaired by Sir Eric Ashby, to advise on the development of higher education up to 1980, reported. This commission, heavily influenced by manpower forecasts prepared by Professor Harbison, gave support to the new University of Nigeria and also recommended the establishment of two more universities in Lagos and the Northern Region. Political pressures within the Western Region persuaded the federal government to also support a further university there. In 1962 the Universities of Lagos, Ife and Ahmadu Bello at Zaria were established. While each attempted in a variety of ways to create a distinct character, essentially the same physical patterns as at Ibadan and Nsukka were followed with respect to large and landscaped grounds, substantial halls of residence and the virtual creation of small townships. The next addition to the university sector was the University of Benin emerging out of the Mid West Institute of Technology in 1972.

With the establishment of regional self government in Nigeria in 1954, higher education had been placed on the concurrent list of functions implying a shared responsibility between the federal and regional governments. By the early 1970s, however, political and economic power had begun to shift towards the federal government and one area where sole responsibility came to be claimed was in higher education. The non federal universities at Nsukka, Benin, Ife and Zaria were taken over in 1974 and 1975. At the same time it was announced that seven new federal universities would be created at Jos, Calabar, Sokoto, Maiduguri, Kano, Ilorin and Port Harcourt. Measures were also taken to centralise aspects of the administration of the university sector and to increase direct government involvement. In particular, a new National Universities Commission was established to coordinate planning of the new universities and a Joint Admissions and Matriculation Board began a system of centralised admissions in 1978.

After the return to civilian rule in 1979, higher education was again declared a concurrent function allowing for both state and federal government involvement. Another seven technological universities were planned by the federal government, in addition to a military university and an open university. Several state universities were also founded and plans for a number of private ones announced. Following the military coups of 1983 and 1985 the federal government has attempted to reverse this proliferation somewhat by requesting state universities to limit their number of campus', disallowing private universities, suspending plans for the open university and merging four of the seven planned new federal universities with existing ones. By early 1986, there were 17 federal universities (including three universities of technology and one military university) and six fledgling state universities.

Enrolments at Ibadan in 1960 were 1395. With the establishment of another four universities between 1960 and 1962, enrolments increased rapidly and by the start of the civil war in 1967 they were over six times the 1960 level. In the period 1970 to 1982 enrolments roughly doubled every four years and reached a peak of 106,331 in 1984 before falling slightly in 1985. Table 8.14 details this expansion

Table 8.14.   Enrolments in Federal Universities, 1960 to 1985, Nigeria

Year	Enrolments	Year	Enrolments
1960–61	1395	1980–81	69725
1964–65	6719	1982–83	92116
1968–69	8588	1983–84	101945
1972–73	20889	1984–85	106331
1976–77	39732	1985–86	104397

Source: Enaohwo (1985) table 1 and National Universities Council records.

with particular emphasis on the years since 1980. The data refer to the federal universities only and omit those students (around 10,000) at the recently established state universities. In 1984–85, enrolments in the 13 universities established by 1976 ranged from 3299 in Sokoto to 13,868 in Zaria. Enrolments in the most recent batch varied from 300 to 1035. Since 1980, there appears to have been a policy of reducing intake at the largest universities and building up the smaller ones. Table 8.15 presents intake figures for four of the largest (with enrolments > 9500) and four of the smallest (with enrolments < 5000) for 1980–81 and 1983–84.

Table 8.15. Annual Intake of Eight Universities, 1980–81 and 1983–84, Nigeria

University	Intake 1980–81	Intake 1983–84	Enrolment 1983–84	
Lagos	5226	3753	>	
Nsukka	3897	2265	>	9500
Zaria	3648	2974	>	
Benin	2984	1726	>	
Calabar	1085	1434	<	
Kano	1356	1856	<	5000
Maiduguri	212	1747	<	
Sokoto	421	1158	<	

Source: National Universities Commission records.

The considerable growth in the number of universities and enrolments in Nigeria over the past decade leads to a consideration of the level of demand for places. Some disagreement over this exists between observers. Both Enaohwo (1985) and Osasona (1981) quote figures indicating that in 1977, 1978 and 1979 only 12.9 percent, 12.6 percent and 15.5 percent of applicants received places. The implication is that there was substantial excess demand. The sources used for these comparisons, however, do not indicate the qualifications of the applicants. Other evidence suggests they are often low. The report of the National Universities Commission planning group to oversee university expansion from the mid 1970s stated bluntly,

... as the projections show, based on the current matriculation requirements, the numbers of available students in the next few years will be insufficient for all the universities, new and old ... and it will be necessary to admit less qualified students if sizable enrolments are to be achieved (National Universities Commission 1976, p.51).

At that time the existing universities were enrolling, on average, 20 percent fewer students than planned. Attempts to boost the numbers of qualified entrants involved the creation of preparatory or pre-degree courses. Since the mid 1970s the situation in the secondary schools has deteriorated particularly in terms of equipment and teaching aids. In 1985, the failure rate for Nigerian students in the West African School Certificate was 72 percent, worse than for any other participating country (West Africa, 16 December, 1985).

The case for a significant expansion of university places based on the existence of large numbers of well qualified school leavers being denied entry to degree courses is difficult to sustain. Nor, according to the National Universities Commission, was the decision taken in 1974 to establish seven new universities a result of forecasts of manpower demands (though these were made). Rather, the major impetus was 'geo-political demands' (National Universities Commission 1976, p.20).

Finding qualified academic staff does not appear to have presented problems for university expansion. The tight academic labour market in Britain and the attractions of higher salaries and available consumer goods to academics in other African countries have resulted in adequate supplies. In addition, an increasing proportion of faculty posts has been taken up by Nigerians as table 8.16 indicates. The student:faculty ratio is currently

Table 8.16. Staffing in Nigerian Universities, 1965–66 to 1981–82.

	1965	1968	1971	1974	1977	1981	1983
Faculty	1208	1288	2245	3560	5190	7980	8620
Percentage Expatriate	53	42	27	25	22	20	NA

Source: Enaohwo (1985) table IV; Ajayi (1984) p.2111.

141

11.8:1. While this is historically low, compared for instance with 7.9:1 in 1975, it results from a National Universities Commission policy decision rather than from an inability to recruit. Projections for the future, however, are less optimistic. It is estimated that 3000 additional university teachers will be required through the 1980s and only one third of these can be expected from existing postgraduate and staff development programmes. As the country's foreign exchange restrictions tighten, expatriate staff may become more difficult to recruit.

Each of the first group of Nigerian universities, established through the 1950s and 1960s, attempted to create a particular identity and set of specialisms. As Ajayi (1984) argues, with the new universities there was not the same quality of initial planning. In many instances, which universities were allocated which faculties does not appear to have resulted from academic consideration. For example,

> Originally, the Federal Military Government decided to establish four new medical schools at Calabar, Jos, Maiduguri and Sokoto. However, in the last few weeks, and as a result of pressures from certain quarters, there has been a ruling that each of the seven new institutions should have a medical school by 1980 (National Universities Commission 1976, p.8).

Similarly with agriculture. The National Manpower Board advised no new faculties, the Ministry of Agriculture argued for one in each university and the National Universities Commission decided on four (Austin 1980). The haste to expand the university sector quite obviously led to a series of anomalies, poor planning and administrative strains. The government's commission of enquiry into widespread university riots in 1978 lay part of the blame on expansion itself and the consequences on the quality of teaching resulting from excessive duplication of courses and the 'thinning out' of the available, qualified and experienced teaching staff. Against these difficulties, however, must be placed the achievements: eleven new federal universities since 1974, an increase in enrolments from 48,000 in 1978 to 101,000 in 1983 and a functioning national admission system.

Most of Nigeria's universities were established in a period of relative economic prosperity. The situation has now changed and federal government revenues have been sharply reduced. In the following sections the financing of the university sector and the financial structure of particular universities are discussed in this context.

142

Education Financing

Financial and administrative responsibility for education rests with both the federal and state governments. Today, the federal government has direct responsibility for 96 percent of university enrolments, 23 percent of polytechnic enrolments, 7 percent of secondary teacher training enrolments and 1 percent of secondary school enrolments. The remainder of secondary schooling, teacher training and technical education is the direct responsibility of state governments and primary schooling is the responsibility of local authorities though largely funded, at least for the recurrent costs, by the states. The large responsibilities of the state governments for education require that they have revenues to carry them out. Between 1953 and 1965, over 60 percent of their revenues were derived from statutory grants made through the federal government and since 1975 this percentage has typically been around 80 percent (Rupley 1981). In addition to these grants, which are unconditional and unmatched, conditional grants have also been made at times. After 1975 these increased rapidly, mainly for the universal primary education programme, but were largely terminated in 1981.

Direct federal government expenditures on education were around one third of total educational expenditures in the 1980s but have been falling as a proportion of both education expenditure and total federal expenditure. They have also fallen in both real and current price terms. Table 8.17 presents these trends and also documents the corresponding fall in state educational expenditures. From this, it is readily apparent that the education sector has come under severe financial pressure in the last few years and that resources even in current price terms have fallen substantially. In real price terms, planned federal expenditures in 1985 were only 28 percent of their 1981 level.

Within the education sector as a whole, some levels have suffered more than others. Between 1981 and 1984, the universities' share of total education expenditure increased from 17.3 percent to 18.8 percent reflecting a relatively privileged position. While capital expenditures have fallen away to virtually nil, recurrent expenditures in current price terms have actually increased, though in real terms they have also fallen, by 50 percent. Overall, the recent picture of university financing suggests that while the real levels of resources have fallen less than for other education levels, the fall has still been substantial and together with increased enrolments has led to a significant decline in resources per student.

143

Table 8.17. Actual and Planned Federal and State Expenditures on Education, 1981–85, Nigeria (Naira million)[a]

Level of Government and Type of Expenditure	1981	1982	Year[b] 1983	1984	1985
Federal					
Capital	602	463	297	108	96
% of Total Federal Capital Expenditure	7	6	4	3	2
Recurrent	781	699	568	581	523
% of Total Federal Recurrent Expenditure	21	20	15	18	15
State					
Capital and Recurrent Expenditure	2562	2156	2447	1745	NA
Federal Education Expenditure as % of Total Education Expenditure	35	35	26	28	NA

Notes: [a] See Appendix A Table A5 for Naira and US dollar exchange rates
[b] 1981 and 1982 are actual expenditures
1983, 1984, 1985 are approved budget estimates.

Source: Federal and state government budgets.

144

University Financing
The universities at Ibadan and Lagos were established as federal universities with full federal funding, while those at Nsukka, Ife, Zaria and Benin were established by regional and state governments. For this latter group, the federal government originally contributed 50 percent of capital expenditures and 30 percent of recurrent expenditures (75 percent at Ahmadu Bello University from 1968). By the mid 1970s, however, the states' increasing difficulties in providing adequate funds led to all the universities being taken over by the federal government. This takeover also coincided with the plans to create seven new universities. While capital expenditures were made to carry through this programme, recurrent resources were increasingly below those recommended by the National Universities Commission as table 8.18 shows. Expressed in constant prices, between 1975 and 1980 the recurrent grant to universities increased by 13 percent while student enrolment increased by 116 percent (Oduleye 1985).
Sufficient evidence has been presented for the periods 1975–80 and 1981–85 to show that despite the emphasis given to university expansion, the level of recurrent financing has not kept pace. The effect of this is graphically presented in a recent description of conditions at the University of Ibadan.

Everything in the university today points to an agonising decline. Students swarm from their hostels where there are six in a room designed for two, into a dingy lecture room where a teacher shouts his notes across a hall of five hundred listeners ... there are generally no course seminars or tutorials ... Without doubt the most affected of all the faculties is the Faculty of Science. For several months now we have been expected to run a physics laboratory without electricity, perform zoology and biology experiments without water and get accurate readings from microscopes blinded by use and age. Chemicals are unimaginably short. The result of all this is a chemistry laboratory that cannot produce distilled water and hundreds of 'science graduates' lacking the benefits of practical demonstrations (West Africa 12 September, 1983).

This description conveys the difficulties facing Nigeria's universities. Since this was written the government's economic position has worsened, foreign exchange for equipment and materials has become even more scarce and the real value of university funding has fallen by 35

145

Table 8.18. Recommended and Actual Recurrent Income of Nigerian Universities, 1973-81 (Naira million)

	1973	1975	1977	1978	1979	1980	1981
NUC Recommended University Income	76.8 74.6	130.7 149.3	204.5 180.3	221.6 140.0	233.6 185.0	290.3 206.9	343.5 288.0
Shortfall	2.3	12.4	24.2	81.6	48.6	83.4	55.5

Note: NUC is National Universities Commission.

Source: Enaohwo (1985) table 111.

146

percent.

A contrasting perspective to the one given above, however, is gained through comparing unit costs of different education levels. This is done, using rather crude figures, in table 8.19. One year at a federal university

Table 8.19. Annual Cost per Student by Educational Level, Nigeria, 1985 (Naira)

Educational Level	Unit Cost
Primary	65
State secondary	219
Federal secondary	1187
State teachers college	730
Federal college of education	2890
Polytechnic	1460
State university	2850
Federal university	3911

Source: Budget estimates of federal and state governments.

costs 18 times one year in secondary school and 60 times one year in primary school. Adding this perspective to the previous one, university education in Nigeria appears, as in Ghana, to be in an ambiguous position – subject to both under- and overfinancing. In these circumstances it again becomes important to diagnose the universities' unit costs. This is an essential first step if any attempt is to be made to protect, and perhaps increase, the quality of education at a time when the levels of government funding are being decreased.

Unit Costs and their Components

The federal government grant for recurrent expenditure in universities in 1981 was N322 million for 82,952 students implying a unit cost of N3882 ($6162). Similar global figures for 1985 suggest a unit cost of N3911 ($4394). Incorporating all sources of expenditures, Osasona (1981) provides an estimate for 1980 of N4508. At the individual university level, Oduleye (1985) presents a unit cost of N1903 ($3392) for Ahmadu Bello University per full time equivalent student in 1979–80 and N2837 ($5048) for the same year at the relatively new University of llorin. The conversions to United States dollars have to be viewed with scepticism. At the 1986 exchange rate, the

147

dollar value of unit costs at Ahmadu Bello would be reduced to $1904.

In a detailed exercise calculating the implications of two sets of student intake a year, Osasona (1981) has broken down the total cost of a projected student enrolment into its components. This has been done on the basis of the National Universities Commission policies and guidelines for funding. These include student:teacher ratios of 15:1 in arts subjects, 10:1 in science subjects and 7:1 in medicine; departmental goods and services equal to 30 percent of salaries in science and 20 percent in arts; research funding equal to 20 percent of teaching costs; and library costs equal to 5 percent of total recurrent expenditure. The results are reproduced in table 8.20.

Table 8.20. Simulated Total and Unit Costs of Nigerian Universities by Component, 1980–81 (Naira)

Cost Component	Total Cost	Unit Cost
Direct teaching cost	138,464,000	1336 (29.7%)
Non-teaching academic cost	116,527,000	1124 (24.9%)
research	24,000,000	
library	24,000,000	
staff development	13,000,000	
Administrative support	212,321,000	2048 (45.4%)
Total	467,312,000	4508(100.0%)

Source: From Osasona (1981) p.16.

This breakdown of costs implies that, at most, 55 percent of the total goes towards funding the directly academic activities of teaching and research while 45 percent covers the maintenance of infrastructure and all forms of student and staff personal support. This cost breakdown can be regarded as an ideal for Nigerian universities with fully staffed institutions and all supporting activities (research) and units (libraries) being adequately funded. Even with this ideal, however, almost half the universities' costs would be non-academic. In fact, as more recent studies have shown, the universities are not being financed according to this ideal or to their 'requirements' as assessed by the National Universities

Commission.

Oduleye (1985) has disaggregated total costs at the University of llorin into their components for 1979–80. To place the results into some perspective, they were also compared to a similar breakdown for Lancaster University in England. The results are shown in table 8.21 and indi-

Table 8.21. Functional Allocation of Recurrent Expenditure at Universities of llorin and Lancaster (percent)

Expenditure Category	Lancaster University 1975–76	llorin University 1979–80
1. Teaching and research	61.5	39.8
2. Academic services	8.6	5,7
3. General educational services	2.0	2.2
4. Premises	16.2	26.3
5. Student welfare	2.3	10.3
6. Administration	6.0	12.3
7. Other	2.9	3.1
Total	100.0	100.0

Source: Oduleye (1985) p.25.

cate that over 60 percent of costs were spent directly on teaching at Lancaster compared to under 40 percent at llorin. Even more striking, if the academic expenditure categories 1, 2 and 3 are aggregated the respective percentages are 72.1 and 47.7. The reality, then, of the funding of academic activities appears to be worse than that depicted by the National Universities Commission guidelines.

Trends in allocations to expenditure categories over time as incomes in real terms and per student have fallen are particularly useful to note. These have again been analysed by Oduleye for llorin University between 1976 and 1982. In table 8.22, the first three expenditure categories of table 8.21 are aggregated to form 'academic activities' and compared with the two other most important categories covering premises and student welfare. Between 1979 and 1982, the percentage allocated to academic activities fell from 47.7 to 36.5 percent while for premises and student welfare combined it rose from 36.9 to 48.4 percent. An

149

Table 8.22. Functional Allocation of Recurrent
Expenditure, University of llorin, 1976–82

Year	Expenditure Category		
	Academic Activity	Premises	Student Welfare
1976	37.8	37.3	8.9
1977	31.6	33.4	20.2
1978	39.6	32.9	12.5
1979	47.7	26.3	10.6
1980	41.4	28.0	13.1
1981	37.2	32.5	14.3
1982	36.5	32.6	17.8

Source: Oduleye (1985) p.27.

important conclusion can be drawn. In a situation of
financial squeeze, the infrastructure and the conventions of
the appropriate levels of welfare services result in the
primary functions of the universities – teaching and
research – being increasingly deprived of funds.

Before policies aimed at improving the financial
health of the universities are considered, three issues
which bear on unit costs are discussed further. These are
differential teaching costs by subject, staffing levels and
welfare services.

Teaching Costs. The federal government has set a goal of
60 percent university enrolments in science and
science–related subjects. At present, 42 percent of
students are in these fields. The justification given for
increasing the proportion of students in science subjects is
that they find more appropriate employment and more
quickly. A corollary, however, is that these subjects are
often much more expensive to teach. The National
Universities Commission has issued recommended recurrent
expenditure levels for 1984–85 by subject. These are
described in table 8.23 and the differences are substantial.
The decision discussed earlier to proliferate medical and
agricultural faculties on basically 'geo–political' grounds
can now be seen to have substantial financial implications.
The unit teaching cost figures, however, also need to be
set in the context of total costs since at least half of these
are fixed or common across all students irrespective of
subject.

Staffing. For the first 30 years of university education in
Nigeria there was over staffing in terms of both teaching

Table 8.23. University Teaching Costs by Selected Subject,
Nigeria, 1984–85 (Naira)

Subject	Unit Cost	Subject	Unit Cost
Medicine	4394	Arts	1413
Science	3402	Administration	1280
Agriculture	3271	Social Science	1263
Engineering	2742	Law	1039

Source: National Universities Commission.

faculty and junior and intermediate staff. In 1953 the
University College of Ibadan had a student:faculty ratio of
3.8:1. By 1968 the ratio had increased to only 4.7:1. Over
the past few years, however, as enrolments have rapidly
increased faculty increases have not kept pace. Since
1975, student:faculty ratios deteriorated by almost 50
percent. Ratios for selected years were

1965	6.4
1970	6.4
1975	8.0
1980	10.9
1983	11.8

The National Universities Commission guidelines discussed
earlier, which vary across subjects, imply an overall
average of 11.7 percent.
    If Nigeria's largest university can be taken as
typical, achievement of the guidelines for junior and
intermediate staff has been reasonably successful. The
guidelines set a limit of one staff to two students. At
Ahmadu Bello University in 1979–80, there was one staff to
every 1.7 students. The guidelines, however, appear
generous when it is realised that only 15 percent of the
university's employees are academics. Oduleye (1985)
reports that a recent commission of enquiry into university
terms of employment identified 600 job titles. The
commission then proceeded to recommend additional ones!
Welfare Services. According to the National Universities
Commission guidelines and the study of the University of
Ilorin, between a half and two thirds of university
expenditures are consumed by administration, maintenance
of the universities' infrastructure, services for staff and
students and other non-academic running costs. University
infrastructure includes roads, power, water supply and
telephones. While these may be provided initially by

government often they have proved to be inadequate, non-dependable and poorly serviced. Maintenance then requires university funds. In these cases, it may be argued, university allocations are not what they appear. Essentially they are transfers from government to carry out normal government functions. This type of argument, justifying the high non-teaching costs of universities should not be taken too far. Both university staff and students have typically received services well in excess of those received by most of the rest of society. The situation at Ibadan which set the tone for the sector has been forcefully described by van den Berghe (1973). Paraphrasing his description of senior staff conditions;

> ... they are entitled to a furnished house or flat at a highly subsidised rate, seldom exceeding 6-7 percent of salary. They receive loans for private cars and a generous allowance to operate them. Medical care at the clinic and hospital is free. Senior staff children receive bursaries for the University's primary and secondary school. For a nominal fee a Senior Staff Club provides a restaurant, bar, TV room, table tennis, swimming pool and tennis courts. Expatriates receive an annual first class return boat passage to England and Nigerians get a special vacation allowance...

Student life is described in the following terms.

> Student life revolves around the halls of residence each with their own Master and tutors, their dining ritual, their serving staff and so on. Originally the rooms were lavish by Nigerian standards and comfortable by any standards. The halls were to be breeding grounds for young gentlemen who would learn their place in society by being relieved of all demeaning manual labour and being waited upon by a small army of servants.

Since this was written some changes have occurred and the physical deterioration of the campus has already been described. Even at the time, van den Berghe wrote of the halls of residence in the following terms, 'As they stand the halls have an opulent, outward shell, and inside appearance of a noisy, overcrowded semi-slum' (p.174). However, the infrastructure of the newer universities remains expensive. Non-academic costs at the University of Ilorin have been shown to be around 55-65 percent of total costs and the University of Port Harcourt has been started from scratch on a 40,000 hectare site (Austin 1980, p.209). One major reason for large sites has been the 'tradition' of

152

the right to staff housing. National Universities Commission figures indicate that for 1982, 4411 senior staff were provided housing in university owned units while 13,364 were accommodated in university rented units or received rent allowance. The rent and allowances cost the universities N12.6 million.

Turning to students, the design of the first set of universities in the 1950s and 1960s as residential has had a continuing influence. While the Third National Development Plan 1975-80 set a goal of moving down to a 50 percent rate of on-campus residence, in almost all cases the percentages in 1982 remained above that figure. Examples are Ibadan 65 percent, Lagos 78 percent, Ife 69 percent, Benin 55 percent, Jos 61 percent, Calabar 51 percent and Kano 63 percent (National Universities Commission 1985). Up until the 1984-85 session accommodation and meals were free. Although no costing of this is available, the charging for meals in the 1984-85 session is said to have saved N65 million, almost 16 percent of the universities' total allocation.

Over duplication of the most expensive courses, over staffing of non academic employees and the pervasive welfare functions taken on by the universities are major reasons for the high unit costs relative to other educational levels. Student:faculty ratios are not excessive and reports of limited amounts of teaching equipment indicate that teaching costs alone are relatively low. At present the authorities appear to be stabilising enrolments and the recent poor results at secondary schools suggest that further expansion is not warranted even on the basis of social demand. With the expected long term decline in oil revenues any plans for expansion at a later date will need to take a radical look at the existing arrangements for university education. In particular, the current 28 week teaching year suggests the possibility of two intakes a year. Even with a stable enrolment, however, reductions in government funding mean that unit costs will have to be reduced or resources increased from other sources. The final section discusses the progress already made in these areas.

Cost Reducing and Revenue Raising

Allocations to the universities have been falling relative to enrolment increases over the past decade. In the years since 1981, however, they have fallen particularly substantially in real terms. Apart from general across-the-board reductions, two major responses have occurred. First, after many years of discussing the issue, students began to be charged for meals in 1984 and fees have been levied on non-degree and postgraduate students in the 1985-86 academic year. Second, the universities are commercialising many of their hitherto non-profit oriented service units and also creating consultancy units and engaging in directly economic activities.

Relations between students and governments in Nigeria have often been volatile and major confrontations occurred in 1971, 1974-75, 1978 and 1984. The causes have been several and complex but a recurring one has been the standard of accommodation and threatened charges for that accommodation. The announcement of increased feeding and lodging charges in 1978 produced widespread riots resulting in eleven deaths. The committee of enquiry into the riots proposed a loans scheme to be administered by state governments. This was dismissed by the federal government on the grounds that ultimately it would have to become the guarantor (Federal Republic of Nigeria 1978).

In the more recent Report of the Presidential Commission on Salary and Conditions of Service of University Staff, 1981, it was argued that the federal government should reaffirm the policy of tuition-free university education and any student admitted to a university should be assured of an automatic scholarship by his or her state of origin to cover all tuition and hostel fees plus a maintenance allowance. The government has not accepted these recommendations and, gradually, is increasing charges. In the 1984-85 academic year both home and overseas students were charged N90 a year for lodging and N378 for board (N1.50 a day). Consideration is currently being given to charging the full lodging cost. A first step has also been taken towards charging tuition fees to home students. At present these are limited to non-degree and postgraduate students. For example, at the end of 1985, Ahmadu Bello University set postgraduate fees in the arts and social sciences at N500 a year, law at N600, engineering and science at N700 and professional studies at N1000. Overseas students pay between N1500 and N3000 (West Africa, 4 November, 1985). These charges can be compared to those at secondary and primary schools. At federal secondary schools, students are charged N240 for boarding and tuition is free while in state secondary schools (with 99 percent of secondary enrolments) fees or levies are charged in all states except Lagos and in most go some way to cover tuition costs. Again, fees or levies are charged for primary schools in most states covering approximately 30 percent of the instructional cost.

The other major area through which the universities are attempting to improve their financial health is in

154

privatisation and commercialisation schemes and outside consultancies. These activities are reportedly widespread, 'Consultancy units are springing up, university petrol stations are being commercialised and hitherto non-profit oriented service centres – bookshops, presses, etc. – are acquiring incorporation status to make them independent of university administration bottlenecks' (National Universities Commission 1985). The University of Benin provides just one example of a set of commercial activities – bakery, poultry, transport, piggery, livestock feedmills, shopping centre, book production, printing and photography. Formal entry of the universities into commercial activities is relatively recent and neither the financial nor the educational implications can as yet be seriously appraised.

SUMMARY

The university systems of Ghana and Nigeria initially shared similar experiences. For much of the period since the early 1970s, however, growth rates have been very different with no new institutions and only small increases in enrolments in Ghana and a massive expansion in Nigeria. Currently, experiences are again being shared with universities in both countries being required to operate at lower real levels of resources than in the past and at levels below which they were designed to use.

In general, the universities of Ghana and Nigeria are today in poor shape if measured by indicators such as reductions in levels of funding, amounts of teaching equipment and library supplies, the severe overcrowding of student hostels and, in Ghana's case, the exodus of academics. Equally, their relationships with central government continue to be strained. As just the latest examples, the universities in Ghana were closed for much of the 1983–84 session and in Nigeria their opening was delayed in 1984. These problems have tended to exacerbate the effects on the universities of the financial crisis faced by both governments, leading to reductions in allocations made to them. Both case studies, but particularly the one for Ghana, show that further reductions unless linked to new arrangements to reduce the responsibilities of the universities will have harmful effects on their major purposes of teaching and research.

The universities in Ghana and Nigeria (and in most other African countries) share many similarities in purpose, design and operation and many of the responses to recent financial pressures have also been similar. Considerable emphasis has been placed in the case studies on the characteristics of university design – including physical infrastructure and welfare services – which have inevitably led to high unit costs relative to other domestic activities and resources. The harsh fact, now, is that for existing institutions it would be economically inefficient not to maintain what exists such as roads, buildings, generators, water supplies, housing, hostels and so on. The question is, rather, how that maintenance is funded and whether public subsidies can be reduced.

In both countries, the universities have begun the process of shedding financial responsibility for several activities previously subsidised. These include bookshops, cafeterias, photocopying services and printing. There is also a widespread move to generate additional funds through commercial activities and consultancies. Universities, in addition, have attempted to conserve resources by reducing levels of non-teaching staff and exploring the possibilities of putting essential maintenance work out to tender. Most controversial of the measures discussed and, partly, implemented so far to reduce public expenditures or conserve them for academic activities has been the reduction of accommodation and feeding subsidies for students. Implementation has gone furthest in Nigeria where tuition fees for non-degree and postgraduate studies are also being charged. Whether these charges and fees are paid by students or by their state governments the effect for the universities is to reduce expenditure. Loan schemes in both countries appear, at present, to be ruled out. The constraints on government finance are not likely to loosen significantly in the near future. Public resources for the universities will remain scarce and pressures to reduce them further are likely. Any attempt at restructuring university financing through dialogue between the university authorities and governments needs to be based on one principle – no further reduction in the level of real teaching resources per student.

An increase in the number of universities is unlikely in the medium term in either country. In Nigeria, 'consolidation' appears to be the theme and enrolments are presently being held relatively constant after a long period of substantial growth. Poor results in secondary schools suggests the pressures to expand will not be great. In Ghana, the situation is rather different. There has been no expansion since the late 1970s and enrolments at each university are relatively low, the highest being 3352 at Legon compared to over 13,000 at Ahmadu Bello University in Nigeria. If faculty could be induced to return from overseas and some resources made available for equipment and library supplies, enrolments could expand in most

156

fields without major capital expenditure, though some would be required. The major constraint facing any plans for expansion, however, is student accommodation. In the absence of a double, annual intake system, new boarding facilities would have to be built. The issues then would be the recurring ones of standards and methods of financing.

9 Conclusions

With a growth rate of over 11 percent a year since 1960, higher education enrolments in sub Saharan African countries average around one percent of the relevant age group. As a proportion of the total population, they are less than one quarter of those in Asian countries. Despite its small size, however, expenditure on the higher education sector averages one fifth of total educational expenditure which in turn accounts for one fifth of all central government expenditure. This level of finance has been provided for a higher education sector based on the central argument that its graduates are required for rapid self reliant economic development. As a result of the recent severe decline in economic growth and, consequently, in government revenues to virtually stationary levels, the sector is currently being critically reassessed in terms of both the capability of the labour market to absorb graduates and the costs of their education.

Comprehensive assessments of the graduate labour market require a range and quality of data which is generally unavailable in African countries. Rates of return to investment in higher education have been calculated for only a small number of countries and while the results imply that returns are generally below those to other levels of education, the data used have often been inadequate in their coverage and many of the studies are already out of date. Recent surveys of government wage structure and the changes in these over time provide additional information. These indicate that while wage differentials resulting from higher education remain wide, graduates' earnings in many countries have fallen quite dramatically over the last 20 years in relation to both per capita income and the earnings of secondary school leavers. While this is partly due to government wage policies aimed at increasing income equality, it has also occurred in countries where greater equality is not a conscious government policy and therefore is an indication that the scarcities of higher education graduates experienced in the 1960s have been substantially reduced.

The existing surveys of wage data, however, are again limited in the information they offer regarding the state of the labour market for higher education graduates. For more detailed assessments, indicators such as reported vacancies, levels of expatriate employment, manpower surveys, unemployment rates and government hiring practices are also necessary. Information of this type has been collected from a wide range of sources for 16 countries. In a very few, such as Botswana, Ethiopia and, perhaps, Nigeria overall shortages of higher education graduates still appear to exist while in others, such as Zaire, Guinea and Mali there are severe problems in absorbing all graduates into the labour force and unemployment is reportedly widespread. In the majority of countries, however, the situation is more complex with a tight labour market for humanities graduates together with continuing shortages of graduates with a science-based education.

Despite its generally low quality, all the available information on the current state of the graduate labour market indicate that employment is becoming increasingly difficult to find in most fields of specialisation. For those occupations in which there are vacancies and significant numbers of expatriates are employed, the cause appears to be more a lack of qualified entrants to the required courses rather than a lack of course places. In the immediate future, the expected slow growth of government expenditure and public service employment suggest a further tightening of the labour market. There would, then, appear to be little case for any substantial across-the-board expansion of higher education in most African countries.

In the meantime, increased efforts are required to both monitor the immediate experiences of graduates and to develop indicators which will provide signals of imminent changes in the labour market facing them. Added attention needs also to be given to analysing the performance of graduates in the workforce. Once a more detailed knowledge of the workings of the labour market has been developed, policies relating to both wage structures and the private costs of education can be developed to influence total demand, and its structure, for higher education.

Emphasis also needs to be directed towards reducing costs. Measured in absolute values, unit costs of higher education in African countries are, on average, similar to those in the developed countries, twice those in Latin America and almost ten times those in Asia. They are particularly high relative to the costs of other education

160

levels and per capita incomes compared to countries in other regions of the world. The high unit costs result largely from the way in which teaching is organised and the level of subsidies. In general, staff:student ratios are low (averaging 1:7 compared to 1:15 in the United States), levels of expatriate staff high (for example, 37 percent in Tanzania), non-academic expenditures high (for example, 66 percent of the total in Lesotho) and expenditures on student support high (for example, equal to 81 percent of the total primary school budget in Burkina Faso). Conversely, in most institutions across the region facilities and supplies of books and materials are inadequate and there is substantial overcrowding of libraries and laboratories. The high unit costs are not resulting in low student wastage rates. In a sample of universities in seven countries, these range between one third and two thirds. Since financial pressures on students are generally minimal the causes are not economic. High wastage would appear to result from low quality teaching, particularly in secondary education.

Measures which would reduce the unit costs of higher education borne by the state include increasing staff:student ratios through the setting of minimum enrolment targets for courses and increasing the flexibility of faculty; reducing student wastage by reviewing admission procedures, the content of first year courses and regulations for promotion and graduation; reducing non-teaching expenditures by limiting the provision of subsidised services and by increasing a range of charges to staff and students; and increasing utilisation rates through the introduction of four term years. In addition, greater efforts are required to improve universities' planning and budgeting systems. Case studies of two universities suggest that unit costs could be decreased by around 20 percent by such a set of measures which would have minimal effects on teaching quality.

While the economic arguments for substantial increases in enrolments in higher education may not at present be strong in a majority of African countries, the social pressures to expand are increasing. Secondary school enrolments have been growing by over 13 percent a year since 1970 and data for Kenya, Nigeria and Somalia indicate substantial levels of excess demand for higher education. One of the reasons for this level of demand is the large discrepancy between the resulting earnings benefits and the costs to the students. If governments wish to reduce the demand or simply to limit their own expenditures, then a system of increased student contributions is one option. A survey of student financing arrangements in 24 African countries shows that in all cases tuition is free and that in nearly all accommodation costs are covered and additional allowances provided. In the extreme case of Zaire allowances are equivalent to eight times per capita income. On the grounds of both economic efficiency and equity there is little justification for such levels of subsidisation. Simulation exercises indicate that student loan schemes could significantly contribute to higher education financing in those countries where earnings differentials remain significant. In others, charges for accommodation may be feasible if coupled with a severely restricted grant system covering the poorest students.

The case studies of university development in Ghana and Nigeria reflect, in more detail, many of the general experiences described in the earlier chapters. In particular, they demonstrate the situation in which the universities have insufficient funds to adequately carry out their teaching and research functions while at the same time maintaining unit costs which are far in excess of those at other education levels and, in relation to per capita incomes, are very high compared to universities in other parts of the world.

A brief examination of the origins of West African universities, the roles they were expected to play and the expenditures these implied explains, for the most part, why the unit costs are high today. This explanation, however, does not by itself suggest ways in which the problem of simultaneous under- and overfinancing can be overcome. The disaggregation of costs by activity – and comparison with universities elsewhere – is an essential step towards this. The Ghanaian and Nigerian case studies demonstrated that separation of costs of academic and non- academic activities then allows a whole host of questions relating to alternative patterns and sources of financing to be raised. This suggests a general point. Essentially, if universities in Africa are not to stagnate and decay, either total funds must be increased or the responsibilities and services directly provided must be reduced. In both cases, given the bleak economic future facing most African governments, public subsidies in their various forms to students, faculty and non-academic staff will have to be reduced and more efficient systems of management introduced.

Appendix A

Table A1. Educational Enrolments and Expenditures,
sub Saharan Africa

Country	Year	Percentage of Total Central Government Expenditure on Education	Distribution[a] of Educational Expenditure			Higher Enrolment Ratio (%)
			P	S (%)	H	
Botswana	1982	----[b]	56	32	12	----
Burundi	1981	19.0	44	29	27	1.00
Comoros	1980	25.4	49	34	17	1.40
Djibouti	1984	11.9	74	26	–	0.60
Ethiopia	1981	11.1	50	28	22	0.45
Kenya	1982	21.2	65	16	19	----
Lesotho	1982	16.9	40	33	27	1.30
Madagascar	1977	24.0	53	28	19	3.10
Malawi	1981	11.4	50	18	32	0.40
Mauritius	1983	4.0	52	40	8	1.00
Rwanda	1983	24.5	72	16	12	0.40
Seychelles	1979	22.4	44	43	13	----
Somalia	1981	10.5	50	44	6	1.00
Sudan	1980	----	--	--	--	----
Swaziland	1983	20.4	51	34	15	3.00
Tanzania	1980	17.7	64	14	22	0.30
Uganda	1980	16.1	29	46	25	0.60

163

Country	Year	Percentage of Total Central Government Expenditure on Education	Distribution[a] of Educational Expenditure P S H (%)			Higher Enrolment Ratio (%)
Zaire	1981	26.4	---	---	10	2.00
Zambia	1980	11.1	52	25	23	1.50
Zimbabwe	1981	19.5	62	32	6	0.50
Benin	1979	35.0	62	30	8	1.00
Burkina	1983	21.7	43	29	28	0.03
Cameroon	1978	16.0	34	45	21	1.30
CAR	1979	20.6	---	---	---	0.70
Chad	1976	21.7	---	---	---	0.20
Congo	1978	27.7	---	---	---	4.00
Gabon	1977	8.4	---	---	---	2.80
Gambia	1977	6.5	60	32	8	----
Ghana	1976	15.5	---	---	---	----
Guinea	1979	----	31	35	34	7.00
Ivory Coast	1981	45.0	36	50	14	1.90
Liberia	1980	19.6	48	25	27	2.90
Mali	1981	21.7	54	30	16	0.90
Mauritania	1978	16.9	33	42	25	0.37
Niger	1978	16.6	52	43	5	0.20
Nigeria	1977	9.6	---	---	---	0.17
Senegal	1977	23.0	46	34	20	2.20
Sierra Leone	1977	16.0	---	---	---	0.60
Togo	1978	26.5	38	35	27	1.60

Note: [a] Only those parts of total educational expenditure which can be directly attributed to each level of education are included.
[b] --- indicates no information.

Source: World Bank (1985).

164

Table A2. Public Expenditure on Education as a Percentage of
Gross National Product and Total Public Expenditure, Selected
Countries and Years

| Region/Country | Year | Educational Expenditure as a % of | |
		GNP	Total Public Expenditure
Africa	1965	3.2	–
	1970	3.5	–
	1975	4.0	–
	1980	4.1	–
Ivory Coast	1970	5.4	19.3
	1979	8.6	29.8
Kenya	1970	5.0	17.6
	1979	6.1	18.0
Liberia	1970	2.5	9.5
	1980	6.1	24.3
Niger	1970	2.0	17.7
	1980	4.3	22.9
Tanzania	1970	4.5	16.0
	1979	5.8	10.7
Zambia	1970	4.7	10.9
	1980	4.6	7.6

Source: UNESCO (1983).

Table A3. Characteristics of Selected African Universities 1978–79

Country/ University	Enrolments	Students per Faculty	Books per Student	Non-African Faculty (percent)
Benin	2578	17	11	21
Botswana	860	5	58	
Burundi	648	5	62	36
Cameroon	7800	20	9	
Congo	4336	18	16	
Ivory Coast	11,430	16	5	41
Ethiopia				
Addis Ababa	12,000	15	21	20
Asmara	600	9	53	71
Gabon	1666	6	24	56
Ghana				
Cape Coast	1421	6	89	
Ghana	3888	7	76	10
Kumasi	2867	6	32	7
Upper Volta	1000	11	30	
Kenya				
Kenyatta	1701	6	29	31
Nairobi	5483	8	64	
Lesotho	1048	6	119	16
Liberia				
Cuttingham	646	10	142	40
Liberia	2685	11	48	21
Madagascar	9814	30	12	
Malawi	1669	11	123	40
Niger	947	6	16	

Country/University	Enrolments	Students per Faculty	Books per Student	Non-African Faculty (percent)
Nigeria				
ABU	8204	8	85	
Bayero	1949	15	28	40
Benin	3841	10	19	16
Calabar	1335	8	38	
Ibadan	6983	7	48	
Ife	8706	10	19	
Ilorin	1310	6	16	
Jos	2515	9	17	
Lagos	9000	12	14	
Maiduguri	1176	9	19	
Nigeria	6860	7	31	
Port Harcourt	400	5	37	8
Sokoto	500	8		
CAR	1861	9	2	
Rwanda	809	5	147	77
Senegal	8753	16	21	45
Sierra Leone				
Fourah Bay	998	6	90	16
Njala	752	7	53	11
Sudan				
Juba	119	3		
Omdurman	1585	6	5	16
Cairo	12278	72	5	
Khartoum	7912	8	26	9
Swaziland	1149	14	36	
Tanzania	2636	5	84	30
Tchad	800	12	16	84

Country/ University	Enrolments	Students per Faculty	Books per Student	Non-African Faculty (percent)
Togo	2200	9	2	75
Uganda	3406	8	129	6
Zaire	28,322	19	16	30
Zambia	3651	10	68	53

Source: Association of African Universities (1980, 1983).

Table A4.   Nigerian Naira and United States Dollar Exchange Rates

	Year					
	1976	1978	1980	1982	1984	1986
Nigerian Naira per US $	0.63	0.65	0.54	0.74	0.79	1.00

Source: Oduleye (1985), Appendix 1 up to 1980.
          Financial Times (various).

Appendix B

COUNTRY CASE STUDIES OF HIGHER EDUCATION ENROLMENTS

Enrolments in higher education in sub Saharan African countries were shown in chapter 2 to have grown substantially over the last 20 years. The main rationale for this expansion has been to replace expatriate manpower and to provide additional trained manpower for the anticipated growth of administrative and social services and agricultural and industrial development. The very aggregate figures presented in chapter 2 are now supplemented by brief country case studies.

Benin. Higher education is offered at the National University of Benin. Enrolments expanded from 600 in 1972 to 4700 in 1981. Of the latter, 57 percent were in law and humanities, 20 percent in scientific and industrial studies and 10 percent in health sciences.

Botswana. Higher education is provided principally by the University of Botswana and at a lower level by the Botswana Agricultural College. The University enrolled 1095 students in 1982. Of these, 43 percent were in economic and social studies, 25 percent in arts and 22 percent in science. An additional 200 students were studying at universities abroad. Some 190 students were enrolled at the Agricultural College.

Burundi. In 1979 university enrolments were 1500 (70 percent Burundi). The annual growth in arts and humanities has been 37 percent and in science, 15 percent. Until recently students spent two years at the university and the rest abroad. The university now provides full length courses.

Cameroon. The University of Yaounde was inaugurated in 1962 and by 1977-8 enrolments were 9488. Fifty percent of these were in the faculty of law, 18 percent in science and 16 percent in letters.

Ethiopia. Between 1976 and 1981 full time enrolment in institutes of higher education increased from 3800 to 15,000 and in science and technology alone from 1600 to 8200. In addition students abroad number over 8000, 60 percent of whom are taking courses in engineering, medicine and agriculture. In 1981, 11,000 students were enrolled in evening classes including 4000 on degree courses. A notable change over the period was the relative switch away from diploma courses towards degrees - the ratios changing from 1:1 to 1:2.

Ghana. There are three universities in Ghana. Enrolments in 1985 were Legon 3352, Kumasi 3088 and Cape Coast 1568. Total enrolments have not increased since 1979.

Guinea. Enrolments in higher education in Guinea increased rapidly from 600 in 1968 to 23,200 in 1978. This constituted an annual average growth rate of 43.1 percent compared to an 11.9 percent rate for secondary education.

Kenya. Enrolments at the University of Nairobi grew from 3148 in 1970 to 5456 in 1981. The arts:science mix changed from 45:55 to 38:62 over the period with the science annual growth rate almost twice as high as for 'the arts'. Over the ten years 1970 to 1979, 8743 degree level students graduated. Overall university enrolments in 1981 were 9069 with another 9000 enrolled abroad. Despite this expansion, the proportion of A level candidates entering university in that year was only 20.5 percent compared to 22.7 percent in 1974.

Lesotho. In 1982 there were around 900 students enrolled at the University, almost one third of whom were in the social science faculty, plus another 1200 at other tertiary institutions.

Liberia. Both the University of Liberia and Cuttingham College were established on their present sites around 1950. Enrolments at both institutions in 1977 were 2107. Over 70 percent of these were in directly vocational fields. Graduates averaged around 300 a year.

Malawi. University enrolments in 1982/3 were 1912.

Mali. Mali has not established a university but has created a number of institutions of higher education directed towards specialised training. Between 1973 and 1981 enrolments increased by 11 percent a year, compared to 2 percent in primary schooling.

170

Nigeria. The number of universities increased from one in 1960 to 13 in 1976 and to over 20 in 1983. The target set in 1960 for university enrolments in 1970 was 10,000 and actual enrolments reached 14,531. By 1977 enrolments were 43,928 and over 100,000 in 1985. Polytechnic enrolments increased from 8000 in 1973 to 35,800 in 1979. The major concern, however, has not been over problems of expansion, but with the channelling of students to what are regarded as appropriate technical subjects. A target of 75 percent in pure and applied sciences has been set but the rate remains still well under 50 percent.

Rwanda. The National University of Rwanda was established in 1963 and in 1980 had total enrolments of around 1000 in seven faculties.

Sierra Leone. The University of Sierra Leone at Fourah Bay dates back to 1827 but received its royal charter in 1960. A second college at Njalo dates from 1964 and is modelled on the American 'land grant' colleges. Total university enrolments in 1980 were 1750.

Senegal. Enrolments at the University of Dakar were around 8000 in 1981, of which 70 percent were Senegalese. The majority of students are enrolled in the social science and language departments and only 10 percent in science. A second university is to be constructed exclusively for literature and humanities and an agricultural institution is also planned.

Somalia. The National University of Somalia formally began operations in 1968. Between 1971 and 1982, 5769 students graduated, almost 60 percent in education. The next largest faculty in terms of graduates is political science with 7 percent of graduates. In 1982, enrolments were 2879, 35 percent of which were in education, and graduates totalled 736.

Sudan. The university sector in Sudan comprises three universities providing full time studies across a full range of subjects plus the Islamic University and a part-time teaching institution offering Cairo University degrees. In 1977/78 the main university at Khartoum had 7889 undergraduates. The Khartoum Polytechnic offering three-year diplomas had 1692 full time students. Government strategy has been to expand science and technology based courses relative to arts courses. Between 1977 and 1979, enrolments in science and technology increased by 17 percent while falling slightly in the arts.

Swaziland. The University College of Swaziland is a college of the University of Botswana and Swaziland. In 1978/9 785 students were enrolled and a further 103 were studying abroad, mainly in engineering, medicine, financial management and agriculture.

Tanzania. Tanzania has the lowest enrolment ratio for higher education among 14 East, Central and Southern African countries. Enrolments at the University of Da-es-Salaam grew from 1814 in 1970 to 3397 in 1982. Recently, the major increases have been in engineering. In 1978 an additional 140 students were enrolled in degree and diploma courses in Uganda and Kenya and 800 in courses in other countries.

Togo. Togo's university has around 3400 students, 20 percent of whom are enrolled in science and engineering courses. A further 1000 students study abroad.

Uganda. University enrolments grew from 1800 in 1969 to 4300 in 1979.

Zaire. All secondary students who obtain a pass or state certificate are guaranteed a place in higher education. This has led to a large and uncontrolled expansion of enrolments at the University of Zaire. In 1980, enrolments were 9927 and a further 10,045 students were enrolled in higher technical institutes.

Zambia. Total university enrolment in 1978 was 3200. The government has laid down enrolment targets of 43 percent in natural sciences, 22 percent in humanities and social sciences and 35 percent in education.

Bibliography

M. Acharya (1982) Issues in Recurrent Costs in Social Sectors. World Bank, Washington DC (mimeo).

S. Adesina (1982) Planning and Educational Development in Nigeria. Second Edition, Board Publications, Ibadan.

J. Ajayi (1973) Towards an African Academic Community, in Yesufu (1973).

J. Ajayi (1984) The Universities of Nigeria. Commonwealth Universities Yearbook, Association of Commonwealth Universities, London.

S. Almy (1974) Rural Development in Meru, Kenya: Economic and Social Factors in Accelerating Change. Ph.D. dissertation, Stanford University.

G. Aryee (1976) Effects of Formal Education and Training on the Intensity of Employment in the Informal Sector: A Case Study of Kumasi, Ghana. International Labour Office, Geneva.

K. Asante (1985) Who Will Meet the Costs? West Africa, 12 November.

E. Ashby (1964) African Universities and Western Tradition. Oxford University Press, London.

Association of African Universities (1980) African Universities Yearbook. Accra.

Association of African Universities (1983) Directory of African Universities. Accra.

D. Austin (1976) Ghana Observed. Manchester University Press, Manchester.

D. Austin (1980) Universities and the Academic Gold Standard in Nigeria. Minerva, XVlll, 2.

D. Austin (1985a) A University at Odds. West Africa, 16 September.

D. Austin (1985b) Uncertainty at Legon. West Africa, 9 September.

R. Bardouille (1982) The Mobility of First Degree Level Graduates of the University of Zambia. Institute for African Studies, University of Zambia (mimeo).

P. van den Berghe (1973) Power and Privilege at an African University. Routledge and Kegan Paul, London.

T. Bertrand and R. Griffin (1984) The Economics of
  Financing Education: a Case Study of Kenya. World
  Bank, Washington DC (mimeo).
R. Bigelow (1978) Impact of Selected Agricultural Schemes
  on the Innovation Patterns Among Traditional Farmers in
  the Southern Savanna of Ghana. Ph.D. dissertation,
  Michigan State University.
M. Blaug (1970) An Introduction to the Economics of
  Education. Allen Lane, London.
P. Bloch (1985) Wage Policy, Wage Structure and
  Employment in the Public Sector of Senegal. World Bank,
  Washington DC (mimeo).
M. Boissierre, J. Knight, R. Sabot (1985) Earnings,
  Schooling, Ability and Cognitive Skills. American
  Economic Review, 75,5.
M. Bowman and R. Sabot (1982) Human Resources in
  Africa: A Continent in Rapid Change. Background Paper
  for the 1982 Conference of African Governmental Experts
  on Technical Cooperation among African Countries on
  Human Resource Development and Utilisation. Libreville,
  Gabon, 2-12 August.
J. Caldwell (1979) Education as a Factor in Mortality
  Decline. An Examination of Nigerian Data. Population
  Studies 33, 3.
S. Cochrane (1979) Fertility and Education. World Bank
  Staff Occasional Paper 26, John Hopkins University Press,
  Baltimore.
S. Cochrane, D. O'Hara, J. Leslie (1980) The Effects of
  Education on Health. World Bank Staff Working Paper
  No. 405, Washington DC.
S. Cochrane and S. Farid (1984) Fertility in Sub-Saharan
  Africa: Levels and Their Explanation. World Bank,
  Washington DC (mimeo).
C. Colclough and R. Murray (1979) The Immediate
  Manpower and Training Needs of an Independent
  Zimbabwe. Commonwealth Secretariat, London.
D. Court (1980) The Development Ideal in Higher
  Education: The Experience of Kenya and Tanzania.
  Higher Education, Vol. 9.
L. Cowan, J. O'Connell, D. Scanlon (1965) Education and
  Nation-Building in Africa. Pall Mall Press, London.
K. Dickson (1973) The University of Ghana: aspects of the
  idea of an African University, in T. Yesufu (1973).
Economic Commission for Africa (1978) Survey of Social and
  Economic Conditions in Africa. United Nations, New York.
J. C. Eicher (1984) Educational Costing and Financing in
  Developing Countries: with Special Reference to sub
  Saharan Africa. World Bank Staff Working Paper 655,
  Washington DC.

J. Enaohwo (1985) Emerging Issues in Nigerian Education –
the Case of the Level and Scope of Growth of Nigerian
Universities. Higher Education, 14.
W. Etema (1984) Small-Scale Industry in Malawi. Journal
of Modern African Studies. 22, 3.
A. Fareh and S. Preston (1982) Child Mortality
Differentials in Sudan. Demographic Transition in Metro-
politan Sudan. Department of Demography, Australian
National University, Canberra.
Federal Republic of Nigeria (1960) Investment in
Education – the Report of the Commission on Post School
Certificate and Higher Education in Nigeria. Lagos.
Federal Republic of Nigeria (1970) Second National
Development Plan 1970–1974. Lagos.
Federal Republic of Nigeria (1978) Government View on the
Report of the Commission of Enquiry into the Nigerian
Universities Crisis 1978. Lagos.
Federal Republic of Nigeria (1981a) Fourth National
Development Plan 1981–1984. Lagos.
Federal Republic of Nigeria (1981b) Report of the
Presidential Commission on Salary and Conditions of
Service of University Staff. Lagos.
G. Fields (1974) Private Returns and Social Equity in the
Financing of Higher Education, in D. Court and D. Ghai,
Education Society and Development: New Perspectives
from Kenya. Oxford University Press, Nairobi.
Financial Times (various) London
S. Gaisie (1969) Dynamics of Population Growth in Ghana.
University of Ghana, Legon.
Government of Ghana (1982a) Quarterly Digest of
Statistics.
Government of Ghana (1982b) Final Audited Reports –
Universities. Accra.
Government of Ghana (1985) Final Government Estimates.
Accra.
Government of Malawi (1977) Population Census 1977.
Vol.11
J. Hanson (1981) Is the School the Enemy of the Farm?
African Rural Economy Paper 22, Department of
Agricultural Economics, Michigan State University.
J. Heijen (1967) Development and Education in the
Mwanza District (Tanzania). A Case Study of
Migration and Peasant Farming. Bronder-Offset,
Rotterdam.
J. Heyer and J. Ascroft (1970). The Adoption of Modern
Practices on Farms in Kenya. Da-es-Salaam: Universities
of East Africa Social Science Conference Papers.

175

S. Heyneman and D. Jamison (1980) Student Learning in
   Uganda: Textbook Availability and Other Factors.
   Comparative Education Review. 24, 2.
K. Hinchliffe (1974) Labour Aristocracy – A Northern
   Nigerian Case Study. Journal of Modern African Studies,
   12, 1.
K. Hinchliffe (1975) Screening, De-Schooling and
   Developing Countries. Higher Education, Vol.4.
K. Hinchliffe (1985) Manpower Requirements Forecasting,
   in T. Husen and N. Postlethwaite (Eds) International
   Encyclopedia of Education, Pergamon.
J. Hobcraft, J. McDonald, S. Rutstein (1984) Socio-economic
   Factors on Infant and Child Mortality: A Cross National
   Comparison. Population Studies, 38, 2.
P. Hopcroft (1974) Human Resources and Technical Skills
   in Agricultural Development: An Economic Evaluation of
   Educative Investments in Kenya's Small Farm Sector.
   Ph.D. dissertation. University of Stanford.
International Labour Office (1982) Paper Qualification
   Syndrome and Unemployment of School Leavers. Addis
   Ababa.
D. Jamison (1981) Child Malnutrition and School
   Retardation in China. Population and Human Resources
   Division Discussion Paper No. 81-27, World Bank,
   Washington DC.
R. Jolly (1977) The Provision of Education and its Costs.
   Paper prepared for the Seventh Commonwealth Education
   Conference, Accra, Ghana (mimeo).
R. Jolly and C. Colclough (1972) African Manpower Plans –
   an Evaluation. International Labour Review, Vol. 106.
J. Ki-Zerbo (1973) Africanization of Higher Education
   Curriculum, in Yesufu (1973).
J. Lauglo (1981) Universities, National Development and
   Education. University of London Institute of Education
   (mimeo).
J. Lauglo (1982) The 'Utilitarian University', the 'Centre
   of Academic Learning' and Developing Countries.
   Occasional Paper No. 2, Department of Education in
   Developing Countries, University of London Institute of
   Education.
D. Lindauer and O. Meesook (1984) Public Sector Pay and
   Employment Policy in the Sudan. World Bank, Washington
   DC (mimeo).
M. Lockheed, D. Jamison, L. Lau (1980) Farmer Education
   and Farm Efficiency: A Survey. Economic Development
   and Cultural Change, 29, 1.
O. Meesook and P. Suebsaeng (1985) Wage Policy and the
   Structure of Wages and Employment in Zambia. World
   Bank, Washington DC (mimeo).

176

K. Mellanby (1958) The Birth of Nigeria's University
Methuen, London.

A. Mingat, J.P. Tan (1984) Subsidisation of Higher
Education Versus Expansion of Primary Enrollments: What
Can a Shift of Resources Achieve in Sub Saharan Africa?
World Bank, Washington DC (mimeo).

A. Mingat, J.P. Tan, M. Hoque (1984) Recovering the Cost
of Public Higher Education in LDC's: to What Extent are
Loan Schemes an Efficient Instrument? World Bank,
Washington DC (mimeo).

A. Mingat and G. Psacharopoulos (1984) Education Costs
and Financing in Africa: Some Facts and Possible Lines
of Action. World Bank, Washington, DC (mimeo).

J. Moock (1984) Overseas Training and National
Development: Objectives in Sub Saharan Africa.
Comparative Education Review 28.

P. Moock (1973) Managerial Ability in Small-Farm
Production: An Analysis of Maize Yields in the Vihiga
Division of Kenya. Ph.D. dissertation, Columbia
University.

P. Moock (1976) The Efficiency of Women as Farm
Managers: Kenya. American Journal of Agricultural
Economics. 58, 5.

P. Moock and J. Leslie (1982) Child Nutrition and
Schooling in the Terai Region of Nepal. Population and
Human Resources Division Discussion Paper No. 82-17,
World Bank. Washington DC.

J. Moris (1971) The Agrarian Revolution in Central Kenya:
A Study of Farm Innovation in Embu District. Ann Arbor.
Michigan. Unpublished Ph.D. dissertation.

National Universities Commission (various)
Annual Reports. Lagos.

National Universities Commission (1976) Report of the
Academic Planning Group. Lagos.

National Universities Commission (1985) Bulletin. Lagos.

H. Naylor and J. Ascroft (1966) A Baseline Survey of
Factors Affecting Agricultural Development in Three Areas
of Kenya. East African Institute of Social Research
Conference Papers, No. 345. Da-es-Salaam.

K. Nkrumah (1964) The Role of a University. University
of Ghana Reporter, March. (Reprinted in Cowan et al.
1965.)

J. Nyerere (1964) An Address by the President of the
Republic of Tanganyika at the Inauguration of the
University of East Africa. West African Journal of
Education, February. (Reprinted in Cowan et al. 1965.)

S. Oduleye (1985) Decline in Nigerian Universities. Higher
Education, 14.

F. Ojo (1978) The Demand for and the Supply of University Education in Nigeria. Human Resources Research Unit, University of Lagos (mimeo).

I. Orubuloye and J. Caldwell (1975) The Impact of Public Health Services on Mortality: A Study of Mortality Differentials in a Rural Area of Nigeria. Population Studies. 29, 2.

J. Osasona (1981) Cost Analysis for a Double Intake in Nigerian Universities. United Nations Regional Institute for Population Studies, University of Ghana, Legon (mimeo).

J. Oxenham (1981) Study Abroad and Education Policy – An Enquiry, in P. Williams (ed) The Overseas Student Question. Heinemann, London.

J. Oxenham (1984) New Opportunities for Change in Primary Schooling? Comparative Education. 20, 2.

H. Parnes (1962) Planning Education for Economic and Social Development, in Parnes Forecasting Education Needs for Economic and Social Development. OECD, Paris.

G. Psacharopoulos (1980) Higher Education in Developing Countries: A Cost Benefit Analysis. World Bank Staff Working Paper 440. World Bank, Washington, DC.

G. Psacharopoulos (1985) Returns to Education: A Further International Update and Implications. Journal of Human Resources. XV, Fall.

G. Psacharopoulos and M. Woodhall (1985) Education for Development. Oxford University Press, New York.

G. Psacharopoulos and W. Loxley (1985) Diversified Secondary Education and Development: Evidence from Colombia and Tanzania. Johns Hopkins University Press, Baltimore.

D. Rogers (1972) Student Loans Programs and the Returns to Investment in Higher Levels of Education in Kenya. Economic Development and Cultural Change. Vol. 20.

E. Rogers, J. Ascroft, N. Roling (1970) Diffusion of Innovations in Brazil, Nigeria and India. Michigan State University.

L. Rupley (1981) Revenue Sharing in the Nigerian Federation. Journal of Modern African Studies. 19, 2.

B. Sanyal, A. Yacoub (1975) Higher Education and Employment in the Sudan. UNESCO, Paris.

T. Schultz (1975) The Value of the Ability to Deal with Disequilibria. Journal of Economic Literature. Vol. 13.

E. Shils (1981) Universities in Poor Countries of Asia and Africa, in J. Lauglo (ed).

S. Singh, B. Casterline, J. Cleland (1985) The Proximate Determinants of Fertility: Sub-national Variations. Population Studies, 39.

P. Suebsaeng (1984) Employment and Salaries in the Nigerian Civil Service: Some Preliminary Notes. World Bank, Washington DC (Mimeo).

G. Sullivan (1981) Some Aspects of the School Leaver Tracer Project — Swaziland. Paper presented at the Development Studies Association workshop on Education and Migration. University of Liverpool, 15–16 April.

J. Sullivan, S. Cochrane, W. Kalsbeek (1982) Procedures for Collecting and Analysing Mortality Data in LSMS. Living Standards Measurement Study Working Paper 16. World Bank, Washington DC.

A. Tait, P. Heller (1983) Government Employment and Pay: Some International Comparisons. Occasional Paper 24, International Monetary Fund Washington, DC.

K. Thompson, B. Fogel (1976) Higher Education and Social Change. Praegar, New York.

D. Todd and C. Shaw (1979) Education, Employment and the Informal Sector in Zambia. Institute for African Studies. University of Zambia. (mimeo)

UNESCO (various years) Statistical Yearbook. Paris.

University of Cape Coast (various) Annual Recurrent Estimates. Cape Coast.

University of Cape Coast (1982) Statistics 1962–63 to 1980–81. Cape Coast.

University of Cape Coast (1984) Nominal Roles of Government Organisations – Universities. Cape Coast.

University of East Anglia (1984a) Statement of Accounts 1984. Norwich.

University of East Anglia (1984b) Annual Report of the Vice Chancellor. Norwich.

University of East Anglia (1984c) Plan For Implementation 1984–85. Norwich.

University of Ghana (various) Annual Recurrent Estimates. Accra.

University of Ghana (1985) Basic Statistics 1961–85. Accra.

University of Science and Technology (various) Annual Recurrent Estimates. Kumasi.

University of Science and Technology (1985) Twentieth Congregation Ceremony. Kumasi.

N. Vanzetti (1972) Education and the Development of Farming in Two Areas of Zambia. University of Nottingham Farm Management Bulletin No. 3.

A. Wandira (1977) The African University in Development. Raven Press, Johannesburg.

H. Ware (1984) Effects of Maternal Education, Women's Roles, and Child Care on Child Mortality, in Child Survival: Strategies for Research eds H. Mosley and L. Chen. Population and Development Review (a supplement to Vol. 10).

L. Weiss (1981) The Reproduction of Social Inequality: Closure in the Ghanaian University. Journal of Developing Areas. 16, October.

West Africa (various) London.

P. Williams (1974) Lending for Learning: an experiment in Ghana. Minerva, Xll, 3.

P. Williams (1981) Universities in Developing Countries: An Introductory Overview, in Lauglo (ed).

M. Woodhall (1983) Student Loans as a Means of Financing Higher Education. World Bank Staff Working Paper 559, World Bank.

Word Bank (1977) Sudan: The Costs of Higher Education. Washington DC (mimeo).

World Bank (1980) Kenya: Higher Education Financing Study. Washington DC (mimeo).

World Bank (1981) Accelerated Development in Sub Saharan Africa. Washington DC.

World Bank (1984a) World Development Report 1984. Washington DC.

World Bank (1984b) Controlling the Costs of Education in Eastern Africa: A Review of Data, Issues and Policies. Washington DC (mimeo).

World Bank (1984c) Financing and Efficiency of Education in Malawi. Washington DC (mimeo).

World Bank (1984d) Cost Effectiveness of Education in the Kingdom of Lesotho. Washington DC (mimeo).

World Bank (1984e) Ghana: Policies and Program for Adjustment. Washington DC.

World Bank (1985) Comparative Education Indicators. Washington DC (mimeo).

World Bank (1985a) World Development Report 1985. Washington DC.

T. Yesufu (1973) Creating the African University. Oxford University Press, Ibadan.

Index

166, 169

Caldwell, J 24
Cameroon: students abroad
33; science and
vocational enrolments
33; university outreach
37; graduate labour
market 62; university
unit costs 80; student:
teaching staff ratio 85;
student finance 100;
education statistics 164;
university statistics
166, 169
Casterline, B 21
Central African Republic:
student finance 102;
education statistics
164; university
statistics 167
Chad: university enrolments
29; education statistics
164; university
statistics 167
China: nutrition and school
performance 26
Cleland, J 21
Cochrane, S 21, 22, 23, 25
Colclough, C 40, 61
Comoros: education
statistics 163
Congo: student finance 102;
education statistics
164; university
statistics 166
Court, D 68, 84, 86, 87

Dickson, K 120
Djibouti: education
statistics 163

Economic Commission for
Africa 46
education and demographic
change 20-26; fertility
21-23, 27; child
mortality 23-27;
nutritional status 25,

27
education enrolments,
primary 5, 6;
secondary 5, 6; higher
5, 6, 30, 71-72
Eicher, J 86
Elliot Commission 110
employment guarantees 47,
64;
see also Ethiopia,
Guinea, Mali, Zaire
employment tracer studies:
Malawi 11-13,
Swaziland 13, Tanzania
13-14
Enaohwo, J 139, 140, 141,
146
Etema, W 16
Ethiopia: child mortality
25; university
enrolment 29;
university outreach 37;
employment guarantees
47; rates of return 50;
graduate labour market
57, 62; savings rate
75; university unit cost
80; non-African
teaching staff 87;
student wastage 91;
student finance 100;
education statistics
163; university
statistics 166, 170;
see also Addis Ababa
University
expatriate employment
39-40, 86-87; in
Botswana 56-57;
Liberia 58; Malawi
58-59; Nigeria 59;
Tanzania 60; Zambia
61; in universities
86-87
external efficiency 44, 45;
policies to increase
64-67

Farah, A 25

182

Farid, S 21, 22, 23
Federal Republic of Nigeria 40, 42, 66, 98, 154
Fogel, B 37
formal sector wages and employment 10–15
France: student:teaching staff ratio 85

Gabon: education statistics 164; university statistics 166
Gaisie, S 24
Gambia: formal sector employment 11, urban informal sector 16–17; child mortality 25; expenditure on higher education 31; graduate starting salaries 53; education statistics 164
Ghana (Gold Coast): formal sector employment 11; informal sector 17; education and agricultural productivity 19; child mortality 24–25; students abroad 33; Achimota College 34; university outreach 37; rates of return 50; graduate starting salaries 53, 54; graduate labour market 57, 62; savings rate 75; university unit costs 80; student–teaching staff ratios 85; student finance 100; education statistics 164; university statistics 166, 170; see also higher education in Ghana: University of Cape Coast; University of Science and Technology: University of Legon
Ghana Ministry of Finance 114

Government of Malawi 12
Griffin, R 73
Guinea: university enrolment ratio 30; expenditure on higher education 31; employment guarantees 47; graduate labour market 57, 62; education statistics 164; university statistics 170

Hanson, J 18, 20
Harbison, F 41–42, 138
Heijer, J 19
Heller, P 86
Heger, J 19
Heyneman, S 26
higher education in Ghana: enrolments 109, 115–20; National Council of Higher Education 112; educational finance 113–15; university finance and unit costs 120–24, 127–33; teaching staff 124; non teaching staff 129–31, 134; student boarding costs 131–33; commercialisation schemes 135; student loans 135–36 see also Ghana, University of Cape Coast, University of Legon, University of Science and Technology
higher education in Nigeria; enrolments 109; university expansion 138–42; education financing 143–44; university financing 145–47; unit costs 147–53; student charges and loans 154;

183

University of Ibadan
167, 171
Nkrumah, K 36
non-academic expenditures
87
Nyerere, J 36

Oduleye, S 98, 145, 149,
150, 151, 169
O'Hara, D 23
Ojo, F 73
Orubuloye, I 24
Osasona, J 140, 148
overseas education 32-33
Oxenham, J 33

Pakistan: education
enrolments 72; graduate
starting salary 75
Parnes, H 41, 42
Preston, S 25
primary schooling: effects
of 9-26; wastage 90
private sector
contributions 98
private universities 97-98
Psacharopoulos, G 7, 9, 13,
32, 42, 50, 80, 81, 82,
83, 90, 103
public expenditure on
education 6, 7, 30, 31,
75-77
public sector employment
10-11; salaries 14-15

rates of return to
education 9-10, 26-27,
44, 48-52
regional universities 92
research in higher
education 67-69, 98
Rogers, D 100, 103
Rogers, E 19, 20
role of universities 34-39
Roling, N 19, 20
Rupley, L 143
Rutstein, S 24
Rwanda: education
statistics 163;
university statistics

Sabot, R 20
Sanyal, B 60
Schultz, T 18
secondary schooling,
effects of 9-26
secondary school science
66
Senegal: public service
salaries 15; child
mortality 25; students
science and vocational
abroad 33; enrolments
33; wage trends 54-55;
university unit costs
80; student finance
101; education
statistics 164;
university statistics
167, 171
see also University of
Dakar
Seychelles: education
statistics 163
Shaw, C 17
Shils, E 37
Sierra Leone: child
mortality 25; Fourah
Bay College 29, 89;
rates of return 50;
graduate starting
salary 53, 54;
university unit cost 80;
student finance 102;
education statistics
164; university
statistics 167, 171
Singh, S 21, 22
social demand 73-75;
see also Kenya,
Nigeria, Somalia
Somalia: formal sector
employment 11;
employment guarantees
47; rates of return 50;
graduate starting
salary 53; graduate
labour market 60, 63;

186

teaching staff ratio 85
University of Abidjan 100
University of Cape Coast
112, 116, 121, 131
see also Higher education
in Ghana
University of Da-es-Salaam
68, 84, 87, 88, 94
University of Dakar 89
University of East Anglia
128, 131
University of Ghana, 64, 68,
110-112, 116, 121;
see also Higher education
in Ghana
University of Ibadan 68, 73,
110-112;
see also Higher education
in Nigeria
University of Khartoum
87, 90, 102
University of Lesotho 87,
88, 94, 95
University of Malawi 87, 88,
89, 94, 95
University of Mekerere 84, 87
University of Nairobi 68,
84, 87, 88, 90, 92, 94
University of Ougadougou
88, 100
University of Science and
Technology (Kumasi) 89,
112;
see also Higher education
in Ghana
urban informal sector 15-17;
Malawi 16, Gambia 16-17,
Nigeria 16, Zambia 17,
Ghana 17
university colleges 34, 110
utilisation rates 88-89, 93

Venzetti, N 18, 20

wage structures 52-56
wage trends: Zambia 15,
Sudan 15, Nigeria 15,
Senegal 15
Wandira, A 34, 35, 38

Ware, H 24
Weiss, L 116, 117
West Africa 89, 136, 141,
145, 154
Williams, P 37, 135
Woodhall, M 42, 101, 103,
106
World Bank 6, 31, 76, 80,
86, 88, 90, 91, 94, 95,
106, 114, 164
World Fertility Survey
21-23, 24

Yacoub, A 60
Yesufu, T 36, 68

Zaire: university
enrolments 29;
expenditure on higher
education 31; graduate
labour market 61, 63;
student allowances 88;
student wastage 91;
education statistics
164; university
statistics 168, 172
Zambia: Third National
Development Plan 10,
formal sector
employment 11; informal
sector 17; education
and agricultural
productivity 18; child
mortality 25; students
abroad 33; graduate
starting salary 53;
wage trends 54-55;
graduate labour market
61, 65; university unit
cost 80, 82; student
wastage 90, 91; student
finance 102; education
statistics 164;
education expenditure
165; university
statistics 168, 172
Zimbabwe (Southern
Rhodesia): expenditure
on higher education 31;